First Meals
Food Diary

annabel karmel

First Meals
Food Diary

Your baby's feeding record, from first tastes to
family meals, with more than 80 kid-friendly recipes

LONDON, NEW YORK, MELBOURNE, MUNICH, AND DELHI

I dedicate this book to my children Nicholas, Lara, and Scarlett, and Oscar—my new baby (puppy)!

Project editor Helen Murray
Recipe editor Norma MacMillan
US editors Shannon Beatty, Christy Lusiak
Designer Jo Grey
Project art editor Sara Kimmins
Senior art editor Peggy Sadler
Managing editor Esther Ripley
Managing art editor Marianne Markham
Production editor Ben Marcus
Production controller Wendy Penn
Creative technical support Sonia Charbonnier
Category publisher Peggy Vance
Allergy consultant Adam Fox
Nutritional consultants Rosan Meyer, Linda Altenburger, M.S., R.D
Food styling Valerie Berry
Home economist Jayne Cross
Photographer Dave King
Photography art direction Luis Peral

First American Edition, 2008

Published in the United States by
DK Publishing
375 Hudson Street
New York, New York 10014

08 09 10 11 10 9 8 7 6 5 4 3 2 1

BD630—August 2008

Published in Great Britain by Dorling Kindersley Limited.

A catalog record for this book is available from the Library of Congress.

ISBN 978-0-7566-3978-5

DK books are available at special discounts when purchased in bulk for sales promotions, premiums, fund-raising, or educational use. For details, contact: DK Publishing Special Markets, 375 Hudson Street, New York, New York 10014 or SpecialSales@dk.com.

Color reproduced by MDP, UK
Printed and bound in China by Leo Paper Group

Discover more at
www.dk.com

contents

author foreword **06** early nutrition **08** healthy eating **10** daily nutritional requirements **12** food allergies **14** kitchen essentials **17**

feeding you both 19

feeding your baby **21** baby's feeding routine **25** feeding you **26** swiss muesli; honey and soy toasted seeds **29** granola bars **30** baked cod gratin **31** sweet root soup **32** bag-baked salmon **35** sandwiches and wraps **36** sesame beef and broccoli stir-fry **38** seared tuna with cilantro couscous **40** pasta with arugula and mascarpone sauce **41** frittata provençale **43** southwestern salad **44** chicken, broccoli, and snow pea pasta salad **46** salmon, cucumber, and dill pasta salad **47** meal planner **48**

starting solids: 6–9 months 49

first spoonfuls **51** first vegetable purée **55** butternut squash purée **56** baked sweet potato purée **57** apple and pear purée **58** no-cook baby foods **59** meal planners **60** other favorites **64** new tastes **65** tasty vegetable trio **68** sweet potato and spinach purée **69** oatmeal with apple, pear, and apricot **70** my first beef casserole **71** my favorite chicken purée **72** potato and carrot mash with salmon **73** fillet of fish with cheesy vegetable sauce **74** meal planners **76** other favorites **80**

older babies: 9–12 months 81

fingers and spoons **83** my first muesli **88** french toast fingers **89** finger food sandwiches **90** broccoli and cheese baby bites **93** tomato, sweet potato, and cheese sauce with pasta shells **94** perfectly poached chicken; chicken with easy white sauce **96** cheesy scrambled eggs; creamy zucchini rice **97** finger-size salmon fishcakes **99** perfectly poached salmon; carrot and orange salad **100** poached chicken balls **101** mini oatmeal-raisin cookies **102** meal planners **104** other favorites **108**

toddlers: 12–18 months 109

energy boosters **111** goujons of fish **115** bomb muffins (banana, oat, maple, and blueberry) **116** baked pita crisps **118** tuna tortilla melt; toasted peanut butter and banana sandwich **119** first fish pie **120** cheese and pea orzo **122** quick chicken risotto; pasta with simple squash and cheese sauce **123** chicken parmesan **124** hidden vegetable bolognaise **127** crunchy tofu cubes **128** ginger cookie shapes **129** orchard crisp **130** bananas "foster"; coconut rice pudding **131** first fruit fool **132** my favorite frozen yogurt **134** raspberry ripple popsicles; strawberry-cranberry popsicles **135** iced banana smoothie popsicles; strawberry milkshake popsicles **136** meal planners **138** other favorites **142** foods my child loves and hates **144**

fussy eaters: 18–36 months 145

healthy habits **147** strategies that worked for me **151** muffin pizza with hidden vegetable tomato sauce **152** chicken balls with spaghetti and tomato sauce **154** pasta salad with pesto dressing **156** nasi goreng **157** annabel's chicken enchiladas **158** mini chicken pies **160** teriyaki salmon **163** my first sweet and sour pork **164** egg fried rice with chicken and shrimp **165** thai-style chicken with noodles **166** meatloaf with tangy bbq sauce **168** cute cottage pies **169** moroccan lamb **170** mini croque monsieur **171** apple and blackberry surprise **172** red fruit rocket popsicles; mango and pineapple popsicles **174** meal planners **176** other favorites **180** foods my child loves and hates **182** notes for growing up **183**

useful addresses **184**
my useful addresses **186** index **188**
about the author; acknowledgments **192**

foreword

It is often said that introducing good eating habits early on will set your little one up for life. Whether you see weaning as an exciting phase or are dreading the mess and the fuss, there is no doubt that weaning your baby is an important milestone for both of you.

It's only natural to approach weaning with some anxiety. After all, you want the best for your baby and there are so many things to think about. What is the right age to start? Is it OK to introduce fish at six months? Is it safe to heat your baby's food in a microwave? What about food allergies—should some foods be avoided?

To ease you into the world of weaning, I have created this guide to help you through each stage, from what to eat when you are breastfeeding to the best first foods for your baby, and tasty meals to tempt fussy toddlers.

This is your personal food diary. Each recipe has a panel for you to record your baby or toddler's reaction and your own thoughts and variations to each recipe. There are meal planners for each age group, where I have suggested weekly menus, and also meal planners for you to fill in, so you can plan your child's diet for the week ahead. You, too, may have favorite recipes that you don't want to lose, so there are spaces within the book where you can write these in.

My career began after the death of my first child Natasha, who died from a rare viral infection, and my legacy to her was to write my first book, *The Complete Baby and Toddler Meal Planner*, which was also inspired by the persistent refusal of my second child Nicholas to eat. It soon became clear that there was a huge amount of confusion and many old wives' tales when it came to feeding babies and children, and so I decided to get to the truth of what were the best foods for young children, and even more importantly, how you could get children to enjoy eating these foods. I have since gone on to write another 15 books, which are sold all over the world.

The message I want to get across is that feeding children is about common sense and a mother's instinct. There are no rigid rules, because every child is different. When to wean, what foods to avoid, and how much food to give your baby, for example, will depend very much on your own baby. My aim in this book is to empower you, by giving you all the information you need to make an informed choice, and dispel those old wives' tales.

I also aim to show you the importance of introducing as wide a range of food as possible to your baby from a young age. Babies eat very well in their first year, so take hold of this great window of opportunity—it will become much more difficult in the second year. Introducing your baby to a range of flavors will help prevent your child from becoming a fussy eater later on, and is also believed to prevent allergies by sensitizing your child to certain foods.

So, get started—be empowered, experiment, and, most of all, have fun.

early nutrition

Babies and toddlers have little tummies, so everything you serve them should be packed with the nutrients they need to become strong and healthy. What they eat forms the foundation of their health for years to come.

From birth until about six months, babies get everything they need from breast or formula milk. Babies grow and develop rapidly in the first years, so it's important to ensure they get a variety of nutrients in the form of carbohydrates, fat, protein, and vitamins and minerals (see chart, pages 12–13). Food must also meet energy (calorie) needs.

● carbohydrates

Carbohydrates are "energy" foods, and should represent your baby's main source of energy. Initially infants are weaned onto easy-to-digest refined carbohydrates like fortified cereals at around six months. When they are older they can be introduced to more complex carbohydrates, such as whole-grain breads, breakfast cereals and pastas, brown or wild rice, and other whole-grain products. These foods provide a range of nutrients (such as the B vitamins) as well as fiber, and have the advantage of breaking down slowly in your child's body and therefore keeping him satisfied for longer. Refined carbohydrates like cakes, cookies, and other sugary foods should be avoided as they supply few nutrients, but lots of "empty calories."

How much should you give every day?

✳ **3–5 servings of protein** 2–3 of which should be from meat, poultry, fish, or legumes, and 2 servings should be from dairy products. Combine your protein servings with carbohydrates and vegetables/fruit.

✳ **4–5 servings of healthy carbohydrates** Young babies need to have refined carbohydrates, but from about

1 year you can start to introduce complex carbohydrates.

✳ **5 servings of fruit and vegetables** Fruit and vegetables should form part of every meal and should also be provided as snacks between meals.

✳ **What is a serving?** There are no precise guidelines on portion sizes for children. You can

estimate protein portions by looking at your child's hand: a portion of red meat, poultry, or legumes is the size of his palm; a fish portion is the size of his whole hand. Add carbohydrates and vegetables/fruit at least in equal amounts. If your child wants to eat more, increase carbohydrates and vegetables/fruit before increasing protein.

Evidence suggests that food preferences are established early in life, so help your young baby develop a taste for healthy foods

Give your child omega-rich food such as oily fish. Research suggests it improves children's behavior and their ability to learn

Make sure your child has enough iron. Sources include red meats, oily fish, leafy green vegetables, and iron fortified cereals

protein

Protein is found in fish, lean meats, poultry, dairy, eggs, legumes (chickpeas, beans, and lentils), and small amounts are found in some whole grains. It supplies your baby with the building blocks for growth and healthy development. It is also essential for maintaining bodily functions.

fats

Fat is the most calorie dense nutrient and is necessary for growth and essential nutrients required for brain function. Fats also contain the vitamins A, D, E, and K which are necessary for many body processes. When babies are breastfed, over 50 percent of calories come from fat. Once babies are weaned they still need more fats than adults, to ensure that they grow and develop properly. Most important are the essential fatty acids, known as EFAs or "omega" oils, which are found in oily fish, nuts, seeds, olive and some vegetable oils, and avocados. These are important for brain and visual development as well as immune function. Research has shown that one of the EFAs from oily fish can improve children's behavior and their ability to learn. Not all fats are the same, however, and some should be eaten in smaller quantities than others (see pages 10–11).

water

Water is essential to the digestive process—both ensuring that there is adequate saliva for digestion and that waste products are eliminated properly. Without water, your baby's cells cannot build new tissue efficiently, toxic products build up in his bloodstream, and less oxygen and nutrients will be transported to his cells, all of which can leave him weak, tired, and at risk of illness.

fiber

Fiber has a host of roles in your baby's body, which encourage it to function properly. Fiber literally acts as a broom, clearing away debris from the digestive tract and keeping it healthy. It also adds bulk to your baby's diet, which contributes to healthy bowel function. In addition, fiber stimulates the flow of saliva, which protects teeth and encourages healthy digestion. Fiber is found in almost all fruits, vegetables, and grains—one reason these foods are so important to health.

prebiotics

Prebiotics are non-digestible food ingredients that aid absorption of nutrients, reduce intestinal infections, and improve immunity. Good sources are oats, barley, wheatgerm, onions, and garlic.

healthy eating

Creating a healthy diet for your child is easier than you may think. Giving your child balanced, healthy meals will set a good example for him later on in life. Here are a few key tips to remember.

● go for five a day

Fruit and vegetables are essential for healthy babies and children. They offer a wide range of vitamins, minerals, fiber, some proteins and complex carbohydrates, and are naturally low in or free from unhealthy fat. It's easy to purée a few different fruits and vegetables together for your baby, and make sure you offer your child fruit as snacks and alongside every meal to ensure that he's getting enough.

● offer variety

If your child eats the same things day after day, chances are he'll be missing out on a few key nutrients. Brightly colored fruits and vegetables have very different nutrients than leafy greens, for example. Aim to give your child a little of everything. Try different grains: Offer sweet potatoes or butternut squash in place of standard white potatoes, and offer berries or mango instead of apples and bananas from time to time.

● keep sugar to a minimum

Sugar not only damages your baby's teeth (which can also affect his adult teeth), but can also impact his mood, immunity, sleep patterns, and weight. You don't want your child to become used

to high levels of sugar and develop a "sweet tooth." If your child is over 12 months, honey can be added to foods in moderation. Children can very easily grow to love the natural sweetness of fruits and vegetables when they become used to them.

● watch out for salt

Don't add salt to your child's food. Little ones become accustomed to salty food and find healthy, unrefined foods bland without it. Children need no more than 1750mg of salt every day, and chances are they are getting more than that in their diets at present. You'll find hidden salt in foods such as bread, breakfast cereals, and even cheese. Too much salt affects a child's body-water balance and can also influence the absorption of nutrients. Don't let salt creep into your child's diet.

● "good" fat versus "bad" fat

Fats, particularly EFAs (see page 9), are essential for little ones, but you want to aim for unsaturated fats, such as, olive and vegetable oils, nuts, seeds, avocado, and oily fish, which are known to be beneficial to health. When eaten in excess, saturated fats, such as those found in butter, hard cheese, lard, and meat have been linked to obesity, asthma, some cancers, and

tips

Keep your child hydrated. Many kids mistake thirst for hunger and can end up overeating when all they need is a drink

Think little and often. Offer smaller meals with healthy snacks in between to ensure your child gets what he needs

Avoid processed foods. These are rich in trans fats, which are believed to be one of the major causes of obesity and heart disease

heart disease in later life, and should be offered in much smaller quantities than the unsaturated varieties. Babies and toddlers need fat, including saturated fat, but it's important to get the balance right. Avoid trans fats, which are oils that have been "hydrogenated" to make them spreadable. These fats may contribute to obesity and heart disease and are used widely in processed and baked food, including cookies, scones, muffins, and cakes.

● reducing obesity

Obesity is a concern for a growing number of parents. The childhood obesity rate in the US has almost doubled for children aged 2–5, and the Centers for Disease Control & Prevention estimate that 19 percent of children (6–11 years) and 17 percent of adolescents (12–19 years) are overweight. Learn to listen to your child. If he isn't hungry, don't push it. See pages 149–150 for tips on reducing the risk of obesity in your little one.

daily nutritional requirements

This chart shows the nutritional requirements recommended by the USDA's Dietary Reference Intakes (DRI). A balanced diet of protein, healthy fat, complex carbohydrates, vegetables, and fruit will provide the vitamins and minerals your child needs.

nutrient	source	benefit	amount
vitamin A	whole grains, nuts, seeds, eggs, meat (especially pork), corn, legumes, carrots	needed for good immunity, good vision, and healthy skin	0–6 months 400mcg; 7–12 months 500mcg; 1–3 years 300mcg 1oz (30g) carrots = 380mcg
vitamin B$_1$ (thiamin)	milk and milk products, eggs, liver, green vegetables, wheat germ, nuts	helps with carbohydrate metabolism and normal functioning of nervous system	0–6 months 0.2mg; 7–12 months 0.3mg; 1–3 years 0.5mg 1oz (30g) lentils = 0.5mg
vitamin B$_2$ (riboflavin)	liver, lean red meat, fortified breakfast cereals, eggs, milk and milk products, dark green leafy vegetables	helps with energy release from food and iron transport in the body; keeps skin healthy	0–6 months 0.3mg; 7–12 months 0.4mg; 1–3 years 0.5mg 1 egg = 0.16mg
vitamin B$_3$ (niacin)	apricots, leafy green vegetables, carrots, liver, oily fish, eggs, butter, cheese, enriched cereal, oatmeal	helps with normal functioning of nervous system; keeps body's cells healthy	0–6 months 2mg; 7–12 months 4mg; 1–3 years 6mg 1oz (30g) cereal = 5.5mg
vitamin B$_{12}$ (cobalamin)	fish, milk and milk products, meats, eggs, poultry, soy foods, B$_{12}$ fortified cereals	forms red blood cells; increases energy; improves concentration; maintains nervous system	0–6 months 0.4mcg; 7–12 months; 0.5mcg; 1–3 years 0.9mcg 1oz (30g) beef = 2.1mcg
vitamin C	fresh fruit (especially citrus and berries), vegetables, potatoes, leafy herbs	vital for healthy skin, bones, muscles; healing and protection from viruses, allergies, and toxins; helps the body absorb iron	0-6 months 40mg; 7–12 months 50mg; 1–3 years 15mg 1oz (30g) potatoes = 10mg
vitamin D	milk and milk products, eggs, oily fish	increases absorption of calcium from diet; essential for growth and health of bones and teeth	0–12 months 5mcg; 1–3 years 5mcg 1oz (30g) sardines = 5.8mcg
vitamin E	nuts, seeds, eggs, milk, whole grains, unrefined oils, leafy vegetables, avocados	needed for metabolism of essential fatty acids; protects cells of the body	0–6 months 4mg; 7–12 months 5mg; 1–3 years 6mg 1oz (30g) avocado = 0.6mg

● A healthy diet

Vegetables and fruit are rich in vitamins and minerals. Encourage your toddler to eat plenty by giving him manageable pieces that he can pick up with his fingers.

nutrient	source	benefit	amount
folic acid (folate)	leafy green vegetables, wheatgerm, legumes, liver, milk	needed for cell maintenance and repair; forms blood cells; crucial to the functioning of the nervous system	0–6 months 65mcg; 7–12 months 80mcg; 1–3 years 150mcg 1oz (30g) broccoli = 39mcg
calcium	milk and milk products, leafy green vegetables, sardines, sesame seeds, root vegetables	required for healthy bones, teeth, and muscles	0–6 months 210mg; 7–12 months 270mg; 1–3 years 500mg 1oz (30g) cheese = 175mg
iron	meat, poultry, dark chocolate, sardines and other fish, legumes, dark green leafy vegetables, raisins, dried apricots, fortified cereals	needed for production of hemoglobin (the oxygen-carrying part of blood) and certain enzymes; necessary for immune activity	0–6 months 0.27mg; 7–12 months 11mg; 1–3 years 7mg 1oz (30g) poultry = 0.5mg
magnesium	brown rice, soy beans, nuts, brewer's yeast, whole grains, milk, legumes	repairs body cells; needed for energy metabolism; maintains nerve and muscle function; keeps bones strong; promotes normal blood pressure	0–6 months 30mg; 7–12 months 75mg; 1–3 years 80mg 1oz (30g) brown rice = 13.2mg
potassium	bananas, potatoes, citrus fruit, dried fruit, milk and milk products	essential for muscle and heart function; helps with maintaining the baby's fluid balance	0–6 months 0.4g; 7–12 months 0.7g; 1–3 years 3.0g 1 banana = 358mg
selenium	seafood and fish, poultry, meat, whole grains, nuts, brown rice, legumes, eggs	required by the immune system; improves liver function; needed for healthy eyes, skin, and hair; protects against heart and circulatory diseases	0–6 months 15mcg; 7–12 months 20mcg; 1–3 years 20mcg 1oz (30g) white fish = 11.28mcg
zinc	seafood, poultry, sunflower seeds, peanuts, whole grains, lean red meats, legumes	required for healthy body cells, immunity, growth, and energy metabolism	0–6 months 2mg; 7–12 months 3mg; 1–3 years 3mg 1oz (30g) legumes =0.39mg

food allergies

There's a lot of confusion about which foods can be given to babies. It seems that every day we hear a new story about the dangers that some foods pose to children. But what are food allergies and how common are they?

Introducing first foods to your baby should be a fun and exciting stage in your baby's development. Yet many parents regard this stage as a potential minefield, because they are so anxious about allergic reactions to different foods.

The reality is that only a small proportion of people are affected by allergies. Approximately 6–8 percent of young children and 3.7 percent of adults (around 11 million Americans) live with food allergies. The difference between these figures is due to the fact that many children grow out of their allergies by school age.

The most common food allergies in children are to milk and eggs (the world over); peanuts (in North America, the UK, and Australia); and shellfish and fish (in Southeast Asia and Japan).

● when to worry

There is no need to worry unduly about food allergies unless there is a history of allergy in your family or your baby suffers from eczema. If this is not the case, it is fine to start introducing foods like meat, chicken, fish, and eggs to your baby from around six months, once you have given a variety of fruits and vegetables. I find that a lot of parents restrict their baby's diet, when in fact it's really important to give them these nutrient-rich

foods, as they need iron and essential fatty acids from six months.

However, if your family has a history of allergy (such as hayfever, asthma, eczema, or a food allergy), and particularly if your baby suffers from eczema, your baby has an increased risk of developing a food allergy. The more severe the eczema, the greater the chance. You should try to breastfeed exclusively for the first six months and then introduce low-allergen foods (for example root vegetables, apples, pears, or baby rice) for the next few weeks. New foods should be introduced one at a time and given for two or three consecutive days so that if there is a reaction, you will know what has caused it. If your child is found to be allergic to a basic food, like cow's milk or eggs, seek advice from a doctor or registered dietician on how to keep meals balanced.

● what are food allergies?

A food allergy occurs when the immune system produces allergy antibodies (known as IgE) to certain foods. These antibodies detect when the particular food has been eaten and instead of letting the body ignore it, they cause an overreaction involving the release of a chemical called histamine. Histamine causes an itchy rash,

swelling and, in severe cases, difficulty in breathing. Reactions tend to occur immediately or very soon after touching or eating the food. This type of allergy is relatively well understood by doctors. Some foods, such as cow's milk, soy, wheat, and eggs, can cause delayed allergic reactions. These also tend to affect babies and young children and can cause symptoms such as eczema and diarrhea, although relatively little is known about them at present.

immediate food allergies

Immediate reactions to food occur right after it is eaten or up to two hours later. Reactions are often fairly mild and can include hives and facial swelling. A severe reaction can include coughing, wheezing, shortness of breath, noisy breathing, collapse, and loss of consciousness (caused by a drop in blood pressure, known as shock). This is an anaphylactic reaction and requires urgent medical attention. Other immediate symptoms can include cramping tummy pains and vomiting.

Most immediate food allergies are due to milk, egg, peanuts, tree nuts, fish, shellfish, wheat, soy, or sesame. Allergies to milk, egg, wheat, and soy are usually outgrown, but those to peanuts, tree nuts, fish, and shellfish tend to remain for life.

nut allergy

Recent reports suggest that almost one in 50 children suffer from a nut allergy, including to peanuts. Peanut allergy is the commonest nut allergy (it seems to have doubled in a decade) and is the main cause of anaphylaxis due to food in the US. The advice for parents trying to avoid nut allergies developing in their children has been the cause of some controversy. Pregnant women with a history of allergy (or with an allergic child or partner) are advised to consider avoiding peanuts during pregnancy and breastfeeding, as well as excluding them from their child's diet for the first

If your child reacts ...

* **Any immediate severe reaction** that includes wheezing, breathing difficulties, throat swelling, collapse, or loss of consciousness is referred to as an anaphylactic reaction. This is rare, but life-threatening. Call an ambulance immediately.

* **If you think your child shows signs** of a mild or delayed allergic reaction, see your doctor, who can discuss this with you and can refer you to a specialist if necessary.

three years of their life. However, recent research suggests that this may not be helpful in stemming the rise in peanut allergies. Some studies suggest that peanut allergies may be prevented if babies were exposed to peanuts in their diet during weaning. The jury is still out and more research is required, but it's safe to say that if there is a family history of allergy or if your baby has severe eczema, seek medical advice before introducing nuts and nut products to your baby's diet. However, if there is no history of allergy then it is fine to introduce peanut butter and finely ground nuts into your baby's diet from six months.

● egg allergy

Egg allergies are less common than people think and children who do develop them tend to grow out of them by age six. Opinions vary, but experience has taught me that a whole egg is a perfectly healthy food for your baby from six months, provided it is fresh and cooked until solid. Children with a family history of allergy and those who suffer from eczema are more likely to have an egg allergy.

● delayed food allergies

Some children have persistent, less obvious reactions to certain foods. These delayed allergies involve a different part of the immune system that responds more slowly.

The foods most commonly involved in delayed food allergies are cow's milk and, less often, soy, wheat, and egg. The reaction to the food may take up to 48 hours to appear. Symptoms can include worsening of eczema, diarrhea (possibly with blood and mucus), and poor weight gain. Such allergies

can be very difficult to diagnose, as sufferers may continue to eat and drink the problem food.

Delayed food allergies are sometimes mistakenly called food intolerances. Food intolerances, however, are reactions to food, such as stomach upsets and diarrhea, that, unlike allergies, don't involve the immune system, and tend to be more of an issue for adults than children.

diagnosing allergies

✳ **If you suspect an allergy**, you must see a doctor or allergist. Do not attempt to diagnose it yourself.

✳ **The best way to diagnose an immediate food allergy** is with a skin prick test and/or a blood test. Both are used to detect the presence of antibodies called IgE, which helps to identify the problem foods. Results of these tests need to be carefully interpreted by an experienced doctor to avoid unnecessary food exclusions.

✳ **The most accurate way to diagnose a delayed food allergy** is to eliminate the suspected food(s) for a minimum of two weeks and see if symptoms cease. Reintroduce the foods one at a time, under the supervision of a doctor or a registered dietician, and see if the symptoms reappear. Keeping a food and symptom diary can help pinpoint which foods are the cause.

✳ **There are many private tests available**, such as hair analysis and kinesiology. Be advised that they may not be accurate, they are costly, and can put your child's health at risk.

kitchen essentials

Weaning can be daunting, but there are plenty of tools and shortcuts to make life easier. Learn how to freeze baby food safely to avoid cooking every day, and a little about food hygiene to help keep your baby healthy.

● equipment

You will probably find that you already have most of the equipment you need to make home-cooked meals, but below are a few items that will make preparing food for your child a little easier.

✱ **A mouli** or baby food grinder is good for foods that have a tough skin, like peas or dried apricots, as it produces a smooth purée, while holding back the indigestible bits.

✱ **Steamers** are great for cooking vegetables, as steaming is the best way to preserve nutrients.

✱ **Electric hand blenders** are ideal for making baby purées and they can handle small quantities of food unlike standard-sized blenders.

✱ **Food processors** are good for puréeing larger quantities when making batches of purées for freezing. Many also have mini-bowl attachments, which work better with smaller quantities.

✱ **A masher and bowl** is quick and easy when your baby moves on to lumpier foods.

✱ **A microwave steamer** with a valve in the lid that allows steam to be released is ideal for cooking fish or vegetables.

✱ **Freezer pots** with snap-on lids are handy and can be used as extra feeding bowls.

✱ **Ice cube trays** are great for freezing meal-sized portions of purées.

✱ **A feeding kit for babies** should include small heat-proof plastic weaning bowls, shallow soft-tipped weaning spoons, a feeding cup with a spout and two handles, and washable or wipe-clean plastic bibs.

✱ **A bouncy chair** is ideal for first meals for babies who cannot sit unaided. Once your baby can sit up, she can progress to a sturdy highchair with safety harness and wipe-clean tray.

kitchen hygiene

Food hygiene is important for everyone, but babies and young children are especially vulnerable to the effects of food poisoning, so it is essential that you take care in storing and preparing food.

Raw meat, poultry, fish, and other raw foods can easily cross-contaminate other foods. After handling these, wash your hands, utensils, and surfaces thoroughly. Use three chopping boards in different colors—one for raw, one for cooked, and one for smelly foods, such as garlic and onions. Keep raw and cooked foods apart in your fridge, placing raw foods on the bottom shelf.

Using a dishwasher is generally far more hygienic than washing by hand as it operates at a higher temperature and dries by steam rather than a dish towel, which can harbor bacteria. Only your baby's bottle and teat need to be sterilized. It's a good idea to wipe your child's highchair with an antibacterial surface cleaner too.

If using jars of baby food, decant the amount of food you need into a bowl and save the rest. Once a spoon with saliva has mixed with the food, you will need to use up or throw away the contents.

Don't leave perishable food out of the fridge for more than two hours, and be sure to use up baby food that is stored in the fridge within 24 hours.

freezing and reheating

Since your baby eats only very small quantities, especially in the early stages, it saves time to make larger batches of purée and freeze portions in ice cube trays or plastic freezer containers for future meals. In a couple of hours you can prepare enough food for your baby for a month.

Once it has cooled, freeze it as soon as possible and label with the contents and expiration date. Purées will keep for eight weeks in the freezer.

Thaw foods by defrosting them in the fridge overnight or by taking them out of the freezer several hours before a meal.

Always reheat foods until piping hot. Let it cool and test the temperature before giving it to your baby. If reheating in a microwave, make sure that you stir the food to get rid of any uneven "hot spots." Do not reheat food more than once and never refreeze meals that have already been frozen.

helpful hints

* **Keep a kitchen notepad** so that you can jot down foods that you're running low on.

* **Keep spares of basic ingredients**, such as flour, canned tomatoes, and vegetable oil, and when you run out of the first can or bottle, put it on the list. Keep basics such as bread and chicken breasts in the freezer.

* **To extend their shelf life**, store foods, such as flour, nuts, and dried fruit, in sealed containers. This helps to keep bugs out, too.

* **Save yourself time** and shop for basic ingredients online.

* **The temperature of your freezer** should be 0°F (-18°C) and your fridge 40°F (4°C).

* **Make your own combinations** of purées by mixing two single ingredients together, such as a cube each of carrot and apple purée to make an apple and carrot purée.

chapter 1

feeding you both

"What you eat when you're breastfeeding is not only important for you, but for your baby too. Ahead, you'll find healthy snacks and quick, easy meals that provide the nutrients you both need, as well as advice for feeding your newborn baby."

feeding your baby

Feeding your baby isn't just about satisfying her hunger. Whether breast- or bottlefeeding, you will be spending many hours with your baby—it's a time for cuddling and enjoying a real feeling of closeness.

Breast milk is the most natural food for your baby, so it's worth breastfeeding even for a week, as your breasts produce colostrum for the first three or four days. This thick yellow fluid is high in antibodies, which help protect your baby against infection before her immune system can start functioning properly. After two to four days, milk production is established and colostrum gradually changes into mature milk (see benefits, below).

Formula milk is made of modified cow's milk and, however hard manufacturers try, they can never mimic human breast milk—it doesn't contain the antibodies that breast milk has. However, if you are unable to breastfeed or are uncomfortable with it, you can still give your baby a good start with formula milk. See page 24 for advice.

● beginning breastfeeding

Feeds can take anything from 10 to 40 minutes, so find a comfortable, calm place to breastfeed. The more relaxed you are, the better it will be for your baby. Choose a chair with arms, which supports

benefits of breast milk

Why is it so important to breastfeed my baby?

Breast milk is packed with antibodies and strengthens babies' immune systems, which is particularly important for premature babies. It is rich in omega-3 essential fatty acids, which are important for brain development, and contains prebiotics that help with the development of gut immunity. It is believed that breastfeeding for just one month has health benefits for the first 14 years of your child's life. Research has shown it protects babies from ear, chest, and gastrointestinal infections, asthma, childhood diabetes, eczema, and even obesity. The composition of breast milk changes to meet all your baby's needs; firstly quenching her thirst and then providing her with calories and nutrients.

ask annabel

your back (you may need a cushion). Keep a glass of water nearby, since breastfeeding can make you feel thirsty. Your feet should reach the floor so that your knees and lap are level. Bring your baby to your breast, rather than leaning over.

technique

It is important that your baby opens her mouth wide and takes the nipple and a good proportion of the areola surrounding it into her mouth in order to stimulate your breast to produce milk. If your baby sucks just on your nipple, she will get frustrated as she won't be able to get enough milk, and you may get sore, cracked nipples.

If it feels very uncomfortable, gently insert your little finger in your baby's mouth between your breast and the corner of her mouth and start again.

one breast or two?

The milk you produce changes during a feed. The early part consists of foremilk, which is thin and white and is a thirst-quenching drink that is high in lactose (sugar), but low in fat. The latter part of the feed consists of hindmilk, which is thicker, creamier in color, and contains two to three times the fat, and one and a half times the protein.

It is important to make sure your baby has completely emptied the first breast (including the hindmilk) before putting her on the second. It is the small amount of hindmilk at the end of the feed that will help your baby go longer between feeds. Some babies need about 30 minutes to empty the breast. If you gently squeeze your nipple between your thumb and forefinger you will be able to check if there is any milk left in the breast.

establishing a good milk supply

Let your baby decide when she needs to feed and when she has had enough. All breastfeeding counselors agree that in order to produce enough milk, it is essential that the breasts are stimulated frequently during the first few weeks and that the mother maintains a good fluid and food intake.

To begin with, your baby will take very small amounts since her stomach is only about the size of a walnut, but if she is allowed to feed as often as she wants, she will be letting your breasts know how much milk she needs. The more often she feeds and the more milk she takes, the more you will supply. This is known as supply and demand.

breastfeeding essentials

* **Nursing bras** These need to be firm enough to prevent your breasts from sagging, but not too tight. They should be cotton with wide straps and a front opening, allowing you to undo one side at a time using one hand.

* **Breast pads** You can buy disposable breast pads to absorb leaks. Don't leave soggy breast pads for a prolonged period, because it can contribute to soreness and infection.

* **Nursing pillow** A horseshoe or v-shaped cushion is ideal for supporting your baby in a comfortable breastfeeding position.

* **Breast pump** A manual or electric pump may be easier than hand expressing. Store the milk in sterile containers in the fridge for up to 24 hours or freeze it.

Milk creates an ideal breeding ground for bacteria, so it's vital to keep bottles and teats scrupulously clean and to sterilize them

Do not use softened water to make up your baby's formula milk, as it is high in salt, which is harmful for your baby's kidneys

Do not give soy formula to babies under six months. It should only be given under the advice of a dietitian or pediatrician

Some women adjust to breastfeeding easily, but many find it hard. If you are feeling frustrated, remember that you are not alone. Call your breastfeeding counselor, doctor, or midwife for advice. It's worth persevering.

establishing a routine

At first, you will find that your baby feeds very frequently and it is difficult to predict when your baby will sleep.

As time goes on, your baby's feeds will become more predictable and she will be able to go for longer stretches between feeds. Once your milk supply is established at around six weeks, you can start trying to get your baby into a routine. Feeding every three hours or so is an average timespan, but babies have growth spurts when they may want to feed more often, and also times when they need to sleep more, so a routine should be fairly flexible. Record your baby's feeds on page 25.

combining breast and bottle

Many mothers do manage to successfully combine breast and bottle, and this is helpful for women who return to work. Once breastfeeding is fully established, at around six weeks, you can introduce the occasional bottle of formula milk so

that your baby doesn't reject the bottle when you wean her. For some mothers, however, giving formula can impact on their supply of breast milk.

You can of course express milk at work if there is a quiet, private place to do it. You will also need access to a fridge, and a cool bag and ice packs to keep the milk cold until you travel home. Expressed milk keeps for four hours at room temperature and eight days in the coldest part of the fridge, and up to three months in the freezer. Store in a sterilized sealed container, marked with the date on which it was expressed.

refusing a bottle

Sometimes breastfed babies will refuse to take a bottle. This can be very difficult, especially if you are going back to work. Here are some tips:

✳ **Get someone else to offer the bottle**, so your baby doesn't smell your breast milk.

✳ **Offer the bottle** when you are face-to-face with your baby, perhaps while she is in a bouncy chair—that way she doesn't expect to be breastfed.

✳ **Experiment with different teats** or soften the teat in boiling water, letting it cool down first.

✳ **By six months** many babies are able to drink from a cup, so you may be able to avoid giving her bottles altogether.

● bottlefeeding

If you prefer to bottlefeed, you will need to give your infant formula milk up until the age of one year. Ordinary cow's milk is unsuitable before then as it does not contain enough iron or nutrients for proper growth. Many women choose to give their babies formula milk, and there are advantages:

* **You can see exactly how much milk** your baby is getting at each feed.
* **Formula milk takes longer to digest** than breast milk, so babies tend to go longer between feeds.
* **Your partner can share** in the pleasure of feeding—giving you more freedom and a better night's sleep.

● position for bottlefeeding

* **Hold your baby close to you** on your lap in a semi-upright position, where she can make eye contact with you. She will enjoy feeding more if you smile and chat to her.
* **Make sure you tilt the bottle** so that the neck and teat are full of milk to avoid pockets of air, which could cause your baby to pass gas.
* **If your baby seems unsettled** during the feed, she may have gas. Sit her up and try to get her to burp by rubbing her back.

● making up formula milk

It is best to make up your baby's milk just before a feed to avoid risk of contamination from bacteria. When out and about, it is easiest to fill sterilized bottles with water and measure out the right number of scoops of formula into separate lidded containers. When you're ready to feed, warm the water, add the formula, and shake them together.

dealing with reflux

* **If your baby** continually expels her feeds, seems to be in pain during feeding, is only taking small amounts of milk, and cries excessively, it is possible that she has reflux.

* **Reflux is when a weak valve** at the top of a baby's stomach allows the feed, along with gastric juices, to come back up, causing vomiting and a burning sensation. Consult your pediatrician for a diagnosis.

* **If your baby has reflux**, hold her in an upright position during and for about 20 minutes after each feed. Try giving her smaller, more frequent feeds too. Raising the head of her bed a little off the ground may also help. In more severe cases, a pre-thickened formula milk or antacid may help.

* **Reflux almost always** gets better in time, and starting solids is often the turning point.

● how much milk?

To begin with, your baby needs to feed little and often and may need to feed every two hours. The amount of fluid a baby needs is generally calculated according to her weight. From birth, babies below 11lb (5kg) need 4–5fl oz (120–150ml) of formula milk per 2¼lb (1kg) of their weight over a 24 hour period. For example, if your baby weighs 6½lb (3kg), give her 16fl oz (450ml) over a 24 hour period. Older babies who are 11–22lb (5–10kg) need a minimum of 21fl oz (600ml) of formula milk a day and water can be introduced too. Give your baby milk as often as she requires it.

baby's feeding routine

Use this space to record your baby's milk feeds as you settle her into a routine. Feeding every three hours is an average routine, but this is dependent on many factors, such as growth spurts and whether it's breast or formula milk. Flexibility is key!

feeding you

Your diet is just as important when you're breastfeeding as it was when you were pregnant, because you are the primary source of nourishment for your baby. A good diet will also help you cope with the demands of a new baby.

Keeping up a good milk supply is not only dependent on you eating and drinking well; you also need to look after yourself and get some rest, especially if your baby is keeping you up at night.

● what to eat

Breastfeeding is one of the best ways for you to regain your prenatal figure—it burns on average about 500 calories a day—the equivalent of running 4–5 miles (6.5–8km). Although you might be anxious to lose the extra weight as soon as possible, you shouldn't embark on a crash diet when breastfeeding. Instead, avoid "empty" calories and eat a healthy diet with plenty of fresh fruit, vegetables, lean meats, fish, and whole grains. It is important to eat a variety of foods, including:

✳ **Fruits and vegetables**, especially those rich in vitamin C such as kiwi fruit, strawberries, and broccoli, since these help boost iron absorption.

✳ **Protein-rich foods** such as lean meat, chicken, fish, eggs, and legumes.

✳ **Red meat**, which is great for new mothers because it is rich in iron.

✳ **Oily fish**, like salmon, fresh tuna, or sardines, should be consumed twice a week.

✳ **Starchy food**, such as bread, pasta, and rice.

Whole grain varieties are especially good and help prevent bowel problems such as constipation (which many women experience after childbirth).

✳ **Dairy products** – milk, cheese, and yogurt are important because they are rich in calcium. Other calcium-rich foods include dark green leafy vegetables, sesame seeds, and canned sardines. Your body adapts to your baby's needs during breastfeeding, and may provide enough calcium for you both, but it's recommended that you increase your calcium intake.

✳ **Healthy snacks** are key because you often want smaller meals when breastfeeding. It's worth preparing some tasty snacks that you can dip into during the day. Try my honey and soy toasted seeds (page 29) or make up a bowl of chicken or salmon pasta salad (see pages 46–47 for salad recipes) and store it in the fridge. You can also buy easy-to-prepare, healthy snacks such as raw vegetables and pita bread with hummus.

● taking care

Eating fish is good for your health and the development of your baby. It's fine to eat as much white fish as you like. Oily fish is particularly beneficial for the development of your baby's brain

tips

Eat plenty of iron-rich foods, such as red meat, leafy green vegetables, and legumes since you may lack iron after childbirth

Have healthy snacks on hand; you'll probably want to eat smaller meals while breastfeeding

Fluids are essential for breastfeeding moms. Aim to drink 8–12 glasses of water a day

> Breastfeeding is one of the best ways for you to regain your prenatal figure—it burns on average about 500 calories a day

and vision, so try to include two portions a week of oily fish in your diet. However, don't eat more than two portions as these fish contain tiny amounts of pollutants, some of which can be passed into your breast milk. You should avoid eating more than one portion a week of shark, swordfish, and marlin because these predator fish have high levels of mercury. Canned tuna isn't classified as an oily fish because canning reduces the fat (containing the pollutants), so it is fine to have up to four regular cans of tuna a week.

I've already talked about allergies on pages 14–16, but it's a good idea to be aware of peanut allergy while breastfeeding. Your baby may be at higher risk of developing peanut allergy if there is a family history of allergy (such as hayfever, asthma, eczema, or a food allergy). If your baby is in this higher risk group, then you may consider avoiding

benefits for you

I know that breastfeeding is great for my baby, but is it true that it has additional benefits for me?

Breastfeeding can help you lose your baby weight since it uses up at least 500 calories a day (approximately the number of calories in a large store-bought muffin, a BLT, or a 3½oz/100g chocolate bar). You can eat more than usual and still shed your pregnancy weight. Also, a baby sucking at the breast causes the uterus to contract, which helps it to return to its normal size much faster. Research also suggests that breastfeeding helps protect mothers from ovarian cancer, breast cancer, and osteoporosis (brittle bones). Holding your baby close while breastfeeding is also a great way to bond with your little one.

ask annabel

peanuts during breastfeeding. Some studies, however, suggest that this may not help in stemming the rise of peanut allergies and that peanut allergies and that they may actually be prevented if children are exposed to peanuts during weaning. Further research is required, but it's safe to say that if your baby is at risk, seek medical advice. If there is no family history of allergy, it should be fine to eat peanuts or peanut products while breastfeeding your baby.

Some people believe that eating certain foods like cauliflower or onions can affect breast milk and cause colic, and some moms swear that spicy foods upset their baby. In my experience, I have found that the majority of babies are not sensitive to what you are eating, so unless you notice that your baby regularly has a reaction to certain foods in your diet, I wouldn't worry too much. Follow a well-balanced diet with a little bit of what you crave.

what to drink

Drinking plenty of fluids is essential for breastfeeding moms. You should drink between 8 to 12 glasses (4½ –5 pints) a day. Try to space this out during the day. This can be tap or bottled water, but it doesn't all have to be water. Drinking some fruit juice is fine, but choose pure fruit juice with no added sugar.

You can have tea or coffee, but try to limit caffeinated drinks to two cups a day because caffeine can pass from your blood into your breast milk. If your baby becomes agitated or finds it difficult to settle when you have been drinking caffeinated drinks, you may want to avoid them or switch to a decaffeinated alternative. Try herbal teas like chamomile or peppermint tea, which can also help to calm and destress you if you are having a tough day.

Alcohol, like caffeine, passes from your blood into your breast milk. If you want to drink alcohol, do so when you know you will not have to breastfeed for at least two or three hours, and don't have more than one or two drinks a day.

vitamin supplements

It is your body rather than your milk supply that will suffer if you aren't eating a good diet. The nutrients in your diet are passed on to your baby through your breast milk. Only the surplus is used to nourish your body, so it's a good idea to take a postnatal vitamin supplement. Your iron stores may be low after giving birth and you'll have an increased need for vitamin D during breastfeeding, so choose a daily multivitamin supplement with 10mcg of vitamin D and 10mg of iron.

swiss muesli

This is based on the delicious muesli that is widely served for breakfast at The Wolseley, a restaurant in London. It should help to keep your energy levels up all morning. If you prefer, you can leave out the extra milk and add a small grated apple instead.

- PREPARATION: 10 MINUTES, PLUS AT LEAST 1 HOUR SOAKING
- COOKING: NONE
- MAKES 1 PORTION
- PROVIDES PROTEIN, FIBER, IRON, VITS B_1, B_2, B_3, C, D, & E

4 tbsp rolled oats

8–9 tbsp milk

1 tbsp heavy cream

1 tbsp golden raisins

1 tbsp dark raisins

1 tbsp dried cranberries

3 ready-to-eat dried apricots, chopped

4–5 hazelnuts, finely chopped

1 tsp sunflower seeds

4–5 shelled unsalted pistachios, chopped

Small handful of fresh berries (e.g., blueberries or raspberries), to serve

1 tsp honey, to serve

Put the oats in a bowl with 6 tbsp milk and let soak in the refrigerator for 1 hour, or overnight. Before serving, stir in the cream, dried fruit, hazelnuts, seeds, and the remaining 2–3 tbsp milk (add a little more milk, if you like). Sprinkle with pistachios. Drizzle with a little honey and serve with fresh berries.

honey and soy toasted seeds

Pack this tasty and nutritious snack in individual portion bags.

- PREPARATION: 2–3 MINUTES, PLUS COOLING
- COOKING: 3 MINUTES
- MAKES ABOUT 1 CUP
- PROVIDES FIBER, OMEGA-3s, VITS A & E

1 tbsp sunflower oil

½ cup pumpkin seeds

½ cup sunflower seeds

1 tbsp honey

1 tbsp soy sauce

Heat the sunflower oil in a nonstick frying pan. Add the pumpkin and sunflower seeds and cook, stirring constantly, until the seeds are lightly browned, about 2 minutes. Remove from the heat and stir in the honey and soy sauce. Return to the heat for 1 minute. Spread out on a nonstick baking sheet and let cool. When cold, store in an airtight container.

notes

granola bars

Flaxseed (also called linseed) is extremely rich in omega-3 oils, similar to the type found in salmon and other oily fish. Wheat germ contains a lot of folate and vitamin E. They both have a slightly nutty taste, which helps to make these oat bars extra delicious.

- PREPARATION: 15 MINUTES
- COOKING: ABOUT 30 MINUTES
- MAKES 8 BARS
- PROVIDES FIBER, OMEGA-3s, IRON, FOLATE, VITS A & E, PREBIOTICS

1⅓ cups quick-cook rolled oats

⅓ cup sunflower seeds

½ cup pecans, coarsely chopped

⅓ cup wheat germ

⅓ cup raisins

⅓ cup dried cranberries

2 tbsp flaxseed

½ cup clear honey

¼ cup packed light brown sugar

4 tbsp butter, plus extra for greasing

1 tsp pure vanilla extract

½ tsp salt

Preheat the oven to 300°F (150°C). Lightly grease an 11 x 7½in (28 x 19cm) cake pan with butter, and line the bottom and sides with parchment paper. Set aside.

Mix the oats, sunflower seeds, pecans, wheat germ, raisins, cranberries, and flaxseed together in a large bowl. Put the honey, sugar, and butter in a saucepan and warm gently until the butter has melted and the sugar has dissolved. Remove from the heat and stir in the vanilla and salt; then pour this over the oat mixture. Stir with a wooden spoon until everything is well-combined. Press firmly into the cake pan.

Bake until the center is just firm, 30–35 minutes. Remove from the oven and cool for 15 minutes, then cut into bars with a sharp knife. Let cool completely before removing the bars from the pan. Store in the refrigerator.

baked cod gratin

This dish uses a very simple cheese sauce that can easily be made while the fish is cooking. However, if you prefer, you can use a good-quality store-bought cheese sauce.

- PREPARATION: 15 MINUTES
- COOKING: ABOUT 15 MINUTES
- MAKES 2 PORTIONS
- PROVIDES PROTEIN, CALCIUM, IRON, SELENIUM, VITS A & D

2 pieces of skinless cod fillet, about ½in (1.25cm) thick and 5oz (150g) each

1 heaping tbsp cornstarch

⅔ cup milk

¼ cup shredded Gruyère or sharp Cheddar cheese

3 tbsp freshly grated Parmesan cheese

1 egg yolk

¼ tsp Dijon mustard

Pinch of paprika or cayenne pepper

8oz (225g) baby leaf spinach, carefully washed

Salt and pepper

1 tbsp butter

Preheat the oven to 425°F (200°C).

Heat 2 tbsp water in a large saucepan over high heat. When the water is steaming, pack the spinach into the pan and cover tightly with a lid. Cook until the spinach has wilted, 2–3 minutes, stirring halfway through the time. Transfer the spinach to a colander and squeeze out as much water as possible by pressing the spinach against the colander with a wooden spoon. Season to taste with salt and pepper.

Lightly butter a small baking dish using half of the butter. Arrange the cooked spinach in the bottom of the dish. Season the cod with a little salt and pepper, and sit the fillets on the spinach. Dot with the remaining butter. Bake until the fish is just opaque all the way through, about 10 minutes. (Thicker fillets may take a couple of minutes longer.)

Meanwhile, mix the cornstarch with 2 tbsp of the milk until it makes a paste, then add to the remaining milk in a saucepan. Gently bring to a boil, whisking for about 4 minutes until thickened. Mix the Gruyère and 1 tbsp Parmesan into the hot sauce until the cheese has melted. Stir in the egg yolk and mustard, then season to taste with salt, pepper, and paprika or cayenne.

Remove the dish from the oven and turn on the broiler. Spoon the sauce over the fish and spinach, then sprinkle with the remaining Parmesan. Broil close to the heat until the sauce is bubbling and the top is lightly browned, 2–3 minutes.

notes.....................................

notes..

sweet root soup

Soups can make a satisfying lunch or snack, and are useful to have in the refrigerator to heat up quickly if you feel hungry. Carrots, sweet potatoes, and squash all have high levels of beta-carotene, a powerful antioxidant. I like fairly thick soups; if you prefer a thinner consistency, you can add a little more stock after the soup has been blended.

- PREPARATION: 15–20 MINUTES
- COOKING: 30–45 MINUTES
- MAKES 4 PORTIONS
- PROVIDES BETA-CAROTENE, FOLATE, VITS C & E
- SUITABLE FOR FREEZING

1 tbsp olive oil

1 medium red onion, chopped

2 carrots, peeled and diced

1 small sweet potato, peeled and diced (about 2 cups)

½ small butternut squash, peeled and diced (about 1½ cups)

1 tsp mild curry paste

1 tsp clear honey

2½ cups vegetable stock

Salt and pepper

Crème fraîche, to serve (optional)

Fresh cilantro leaves, for garnish (optional)

Heat the oil in a large pan and sauté the vegetables until they start to soften, about 10–15 minutes. Stir in the curry paste and honey, and cook for 1 minute. Add the stock and bring to a simmer, then cook uncovered until the vegetables are very tender, 20–25 minutes.

Let cool slightly before pouring into a blender and combining until smooth (be careful when blending hot liquids). Season to taste. Warm gently before serving. This dish is particularly nice if you top each bowl of soup with a small spoonful of crème fraîche and a few cilantro leaves.

> Carrots are one of nature's top sources of vitamin C, and, interestingly, cooked carrots have twice the antioxidant power of raw carrots

bag-baked salmon

Oily fish such as salmon contains plenty of omega-3 fatty acids, which are good for both you and your baby. These bags can be assembled earlier in the day and then be kept in the refrigerator until needed.

- PREPARATION: 10–15 MINUTES
- COOKING: ABOUT 15 MINUTES
- MAKES 2 PORTIONS
- PROVIDES PROTEIN, OMEGA-3s, IRON, SELENIUM, BETA-CAROTENE, VIT E

¼ red bell pepper, thinly sliced

2 fresh shiitake or oyster mushrooms, stems removed and finely sliced

2 pieces of salmon fillet, about 1in (2.5cm) thick and 6oz (175g) each

2 large scallions, finely sliced

½ tsp grated fresh ginger

2 tsp soy sauce

1 tbsp mirin

½ tsp sugar

Preheat the oven to 400°F (200°C). Cut out two rectangles of foil about 16 x 12in (40 x 30cm), and two rectangles of parchment paper of equal size.

Lay the foil rectangles on a flat surface and put a piece of parchment paper on top of each. Mix the red pepper and mushrooms together and spoon half of the mixture into the center of each piece of parchment paper. Sit the salmon on top of the vegetables and sprinkle the scallions over the fish. Mix together the ginger, soy sauce, mirin, and sugar until the sugar has dissolved, then carefully spoon this over the salmon.

Bring the long sides of the foil and parchment paper together over the salmon, and roll and fold over to seal. Twist and scrunch the ends together so that the salmon is completely enclosed. Set the bags on a baking sheet. Bake until the salmon is opaque all the way through and flakes when pressed with a fork, about 15 minutes. Undo the bags and transfer the salmon to plates, then spoon the vegetables and sauce over the fish.

> Oily fish is the best source of essential fatty acids. Juices, yogurts, and cereal bars are often enriched with omega-3s, but these are mostly plant-derived, and are less beneficial

notes

sandwiches and wraps

If you are out and about during the day, or going to work, why not prepare a sandwich or wrap in the morning and take it with you? They make fast and satisfying lunches or snacks, especially if you pack them full of crisp salad and lean meats. Adding a tasty dressing means that they won't let you down on flavor either. Here are a few of my favorite sandwich and wrap ideas.

turkey and tomato sandwich with honey-mustard mayo

I like arugula, which has a peppery bite, but if you would prefer something different, try baby spinach leaves instead. This also makes a nice filling for a flour tortilla wrap.

- PREPARATION: 5 MINUTES
- COOKING: NONE
- MAKES 1 PORTION
- PROVIDES PROTEIN, FIBER, IRON, ZINC, SELENIUM, VITS A, B_1, B_2, C, & E

2 tbsp mayonnaise (low-fat is fine)

1 tsp whole-grain mustard (or to taste)

½ tsp clear honey

2 slices whole-grain bread

2 thin slices cooked turkey breast (about 2oz/55g)

1 medium tomato, thinly sliced

Handful of small arugula leaves

Salt and pepper

Mix the mayonnaise, mustard, and honey together and spread half over one side of one of the slices of bread. Lay the turkey on top, followed by the tomato and arugula. Season to taste with salt and pepper. Spread the remaining mayonnaise over the second slice of bread and press down on the arugula. Cut the sandwich in half to serve.

" Turkey contains more zinc than chicken, and zinc helps to boost the immune system. It also contains tryptophan, which the body uses to make the "happy" chemical serotonin "

chicken and avocado wrap

This is also good as a sandwich made with multigrain bread.

- PREPARATION: 5 MINUTES
- COOKING: NONE
- MAKES 1 PORTION
- PROVIDES PROTEIN, FIBER, IRON, ZINC, SELENIUM, VITS A & E

1½ tbsp mayonnaise (low-fat is fine)

2 tsp lemon juice

1 flour tortilla wrap

Small handful of cress or alfalfa

2 thin slices cooked chicken breast (about 2oz/55g)

½ small (Hass) avocado, thinly sliced

Salt and pepper

Mix the mayonnaise and lemon juice together in a small bowl. Warm the tortilla in the microwave for 5–10 seconds until soft, then spread the lemon mayonnaise over it. Sprinkle the cress down the center and lay the chicken on top, followed by the avocado. Season with a little salt and pepper, then roll up the wrap and cut in half. Secure each half with a toothpick.

chinese-style beef wrap

This wrap reminds me of one of my favorite Chinese dishes—Peking duck. Beansprouts and lettuce make a super-quick filling, but if you have extra time, replace them with a finely sliced scallion and a handful of matchstick-sized strips of cucumber.

- PREPARATION: 5 MINUTES
- COOKING: NONE
- MAKES 1 PORTION
- PROVIDES PROTEIN, FIBER, IRON, ZINC, SELENIUM, VITS C & E

1 tbsp mayonnaise (low-fat is fine)

2 tsp plum sauce

Large squeeze of lemon juice

1 flour tortilla wrap

2 thin slices roast beef (about 2oz/55g), or cooked chicken

2 heaping tbsp beansprouts

¼ cup shredded lettuce

Salt and pepper

Mix together the mayonnaise, plum sauce, and lemon juice. Warm the tortilla in the microwave for 10 seconds, then spread the mayonnaise mixture over it. Lay the beef (or chicken) down the center and scatter the beansprouts and lettuce on top. Season with a little salt and pepper, then roll up and cut in half. Secure each half with a toothpick.

notes

notes ....

sesame beef and broccoli stir-fry

You can prepare all the ingredients for this stir-fry in advance and keep them, covered, in the refrigerator until ready to cook. It will then take only a few minutes to have supper on the table.

- PREPARATION: 10 MINUTES
- COOKING: 15 MINUTES
- MAKES 2 PORTIONS
- PROVIDES PROTEIN, IRON, SELENIUM, ZINC, CALCIUM, FOLATE, VITS A & B$_{12}$

4oz (115g) medium egg noodles

1 tbsp plus 1 tsp sunflower oil

1 tsp toasted sesame oil

1 tbsp sesame seeds

½ hot red chili, seeded and thinly sliced (optional)

1 clove garlic, crushed

½ tsp grated fresh ginger

5oz (150g) small broccoli florets (about ⅔ cup)

8oz (225g) boneless sirloin steak or filet mignon, cut into small strips

2 large scallions, thinly sliced

¼ cup oyster sauce

1 tsp sugar

1½ tbsp soy sauce (or to taste)

Cook the noodles according to package directions. Drain and rinse with cold water, then toss with 1 tsp sunflower oil and the sesame oil. Set aside.

Put the sesame seeds in a wok set over medium heat and toast them for 1–2 minutes. Transfer to a bowl and set aside. Add the remaining sunflower oil to the wok along with the sliced chile (if using), garlic, and ginger. Cook for 1 minute, then add the broccoli and beef. Stir-fry until the broccoli is tender and the beef is cooked, about 6 minutes.

Add the noodles, scallions, oyster sauce, sugar, and soy sauce, and cook for 2 minutes longer. Sprinkle with the sesame seeds before serving.

" Many young moms are deficient in iron, which leaves them feeling tired. Red meat provides the best source of iron, helping to boost energy and concentration. "

notes...
....
....
....
....
....
....
....
....
....
....
....
....
....
....
....
....
....
....
....
....
....
....
....
....

seared tuna with cilantro couscous

Tuna and other oily fish are the best sources of omega-3 essential fatty acids, which are very important for the development of a baby's eyesight and brain (a baby's brain triples in size in the first year). Omega-3s can potentially be passed to your baby through your breast milk, so try to eat two portions of oily fish a week.

- PREPARATION: 10 MINUTES, PLUS 1 HOUR MARINATING
- COOKING: 5 MINUTES, PLUS 5 MINUTES STANDING
- MAKES 2 PORTIONS
- PROVIDES PROTEIN, OMEGA-3s, IRON, SELENIUM, VITS B_1, B_3,& C

2 tbsp soy sauce

2 tbsp mirin

1 tbsp light brown sugar

1 fresh tuna steak, about ⅝in (1½cm) thick and weighing 8oz (225g)

1 tbsp sunflower oil

Couscous

⅔ cup couscous

1 tbsp olive oil

Scant 1 cup hot vegetable stock

2 scallions, thinly sliced

Handful of fresh cilantro leaves, coarsely chopped

1 tbsp lime juice (or to taste)

Salt and pepper

Mix the soy sauce, mirin, and sugar together in a large dish. Add the tuna and turn to coat. Let marinate in the refrigerator for 1 hour, turning the tuna over halfway through. (Don't marinate longer or the tuna will turn mushy.)

Meanwhile, put the couscous in a large bowl and stir in the olive oil, followed by the hot stock. Cover the bowl tightly with plastic wrap and let stand for 5 minutes until the stock has been absorbed. Uncover and fluff up the couscous with a fork, then gently stir in the scallions, cilantro, and lime juice. Season with salt and pepper. Spread out on two plates.

Put a ridged grill pan over high heat and brush with sunflower oil. Remove the tuna from the marinade (reserve the marinade) and pat dry with paper towels. Sear on the hot grill pan for 2 minutes on each side for medium-cooked tuna (thinner pieces of tuna will cook more quickly). Rest the tuna on a plate for 5 minutes.

Put the reserved marinade in a small saucepan with 2 tbsp water. Bring up to a boil and simmer for 1 minute to make a sauce. Slice the tuna and lay it on the couscous, then drizzle the sauce over the top.

pasta with arugula and mascarpone sauce

This sauce is so quick that you can make it while the pasta is cooking. If you like garlic, then add a small clove to the food processor with the arugula. You can also toss in a handful of halved cherry tomatoes at the end for a bit of bright color contrast.

- PREPARATION: 10 MINUTES
- COOKING: 8–10 MINUTES
- MAKES 2 PORTIONS
- PROVIDES PROTEIN, CALCIUM, FOLATE, VITS A, C, D, & E

8oz (225g) bowtie, spiral, or corkscrew pasta (about 1½ cups)

4oz (115g) arugula (about 4 handfuls)

½ cup mascarpone

¼ cup freshly grated Parmesan cheese, plus extra to serve

2 tsp lemon juice

Salt and pepper

Cook the pasta according to package directions. Meanwhile, put the arugula in the bowl of a food processor and process, pulsing the machine on and off, until finely chopped. Add the mascarpone, Parmesan, and lemon juice, and process again to combine (if the mascarpone is very thick and creamy, you might need to add 1 tbsp milk). Season to taste with salt and pepper.

Drain the pasta well and return to the pan. Add the arugula sauce and toss to coat the pasta. Serve with extra Parmesan, if desired.

notes.....................

frittata provençale

I may be mixing my countries a bit in the title here, but a flat omelet bolstered with summer vegetables makes a lovely quick lunch or light supper. This is also good cold, so keep leftovers in the refrigerator for a time when you need a quick snack.

- PREPARATION: 20 MINUTES
- COOKING: 25 MINUTES
- MAKES 4–6 PORTIONS
- PROVIDES PROTEIN, BETA-CAROTENE, FOLATE, VITS C, D, & E

3–4 boiling potatoes

6 eggs

1 tsp chopped fresh thyme leaves (or other herbs such as chives, parsley, tarragon, and chervil)

¼ cup crème fraîche or heavy cream

Salt and pepper

2 tbsp olive oil

1 small red onion, thinly sliced

½ red bell pepper, thinly sliced

1 medium zucchini, thinly sliced

1 clove garlic, crushed

1 cup shredded Gruyère cheese

2 tbsp freshly grated Parmesan cheese

Cook the potatoes in a pan of boiling salted water until just tender, about 12 minutes. When cool enough to handle, cut into slices and set aside. Beat the eggs in a bowl with the thyme and crème fraîche. Season well with salt and pepper and set aside.

Heat the oil in a medium nonstick frying pan (8–9in/20–23cm in diameter) and sauté the onion, red pepper, and zucchini until just soft, 8–10 minutes. Add the garlic and potatoes and cook for another minute. Spread out the vegetables in the pan, then pour in the egg mixture. Cook, stirring occasionally, for 2–3 minutes, then leave the frittata to cook until it is just set underneath, but still wobbly on top, 6–7 minutes longer. Meanwhile, preheat the broiler.

Scatter the cheeses over the frittata and broil, 2–3in (5–8cm) from the heat, until the cheese is golden brown and bubbly and the frittata has set on top, about 2–4 minutes. Remove from the broiler and let stand for 5 minutes.

Loosen the frittata from the pan using a spatula, then slide out onto a large plate. Cut into wedges to serve.

notes..

" Buy omega-3-enriched eggs, laid by hens that are fed oil-rich seeds. Research shows that these may be good for babies' brain and eye development "

notes

southwestern salad

Corn and beans contain complementary amino acids, which means that when they are combined, they are a great source of protein. Corn is also rich in folate. Crunchy salads tossed in tangy dressings are popular in Southern California and the Southwest.

- PREPARATION: 10 MINUTES
- COOKING: NONE
- MAKES 2 PORTIONS
- PROVIDES PROTEIN, FIBER, CALCIUM, IRON, BETA-CAROTENE, VITS B_2, C, & E

2 tbsp mayonnaise (low-fat is fine)

2 tbsp plain yogurt

1 tsp lemon juice

1–2 tbsp milk

2 tsp chopped fresh dill or cilantro

Salt and pepper

1 cup canned corn, drained

1 cup canned red kidney beans, drained and rinsed

½ red bell pepper, diced

2 scallions, thinly sliced

¼ head iceberg or ½ head romaine

1 avocado, sliced

In a large bowl, whisk together the mayonnaise, yogurt, and lemon juice. Whisk in enough milk to give a coating consistency, then stir in the dill and season with salt and pepper. Add the corn, beans, red pepper, and scallions, and toss to coat in the dressing. Cover and chill until needed.

Just before serving, put the lettuce in the bottom of a salad bowl, add a few spoonfuls of the mixture, and arrange the avocado slices on top.

notes..
....
....
....
....
....
....
....
....
....
....
....
....
....
....
....
....
....
....

chicken, broccoli, and snow pea pasta salad

Since broccoli is rich in a wide range of nutrients, it is king of the superfood vegetables. It also helps strengthen the immune system and is a major force in fighting various forms of cancer.

- PREPARATION: 10 MINUTES
- COOKING: 10 MINUTES
- MAKES 2 PORTIONS
- PROVIDES PROTEIN, OMEGA-3s, IRON, ZINC, SELENIUM, FOLATE, VITS A & C

4oz (115g) pasta spirals (about ¾ cup)

½ cup small broccoli florets

¼ cup snow peas

3 tbsp sunflower oil

½ tsp toasted sesame oil

2 tsp rice wine vinegar

2 tsp clear honey

2 tsp soy sauce

4oz (115g) cooked chicken, thinly sliced (½–¾ cup)

3 tbsp pumpkin seeds

Cook the pasta according to package directions, adding the broccoli and snow peas 2 minutes before the end of the cooking time. Drain and immediately rinse well with cold water. Drain well again.

Whisk together the oils, vinegar, honey, and soy sauce in a large bowl. Add the pasta and vegetables and toss to coat. Cover and refrigerate until needed. Just before serving, add the chicken and toss again, then sprinkle with the pumpkin seeds.

salmon, cucumber, and dill pasta salad

A well-balanced meal should contain a combination of proteins and carbohydrates to enable the body to repair and refuel. This salad contains both, and the pasta is fairly low on the glycemic index, which means that it breaks down slowly and helps to keep energy levels steady. Salmon takes only a few minutes to cook in the microwave, so this is quick and easy to prepare.

- PREPARATION: 10 MINUTES
- COOKING: 10–12 MINUTES
- MAKES 2 PORTIONS
- PROVIDES PROTEIN, OMEGA-3s, IRON, SELENIUM, VITS A, C, & E

4oz (115g) bowtie pasta (about ¾ cup)

⅓ English cucumber

2 tbsp crème fraîche

1 tbsp mayonnaise (low-fat is fine)

2–3 tsp lemon juice (to taste)

2 tsp chopped fresh dill

2 scallions, thinly sliced

Salt and pepper

5oz (150g) salmon fillet, cooked (see below), skinned, and flaked

Cook the pasta according to package directions. Drain and rinse with cold water, then drain again. While the pasta is cooking, peel the cucumber, cut in half lengthwise, and scoop out the seeds with a spoon. Thinly slice the cucumber.

Mix the crème fraîche, mayonnaise, lemon juice, and dill together in a large bowl. Add the pasta, cucumber, and scallions. Toss well and season to taste with salt and pepper. Cover and refrigerate until needed. Just before serving, scatter the flaked salmon over the top.

Note: To cook the salmon in the microwave, put it in a fairly deep glass dish and season with a little salt and pepper. Add 3 tbsp water plus a squeeze of lemon juice. Cover and microwave on high until the salmon is opaque all the way through and flakes easily when pressed with a fork, 2–3 minutes.

Alternatively, poach the salmon: Put 2 cups fish or vegetable stock in a medium saucepan and bring to a simmer. Add the salmon, flesh side down, and cook at a very gentle simmer for 7 minutes. Turn the salmon over and cook until the fish is opaque all the way through and breaks into large flakes when pressed with a fork, 4–5 minutes longer. (Thicker pieces of salmon may take a few more minutes.)

notes

meal planner: feeding you

Below are some healthy meal and snack suggestions while you're breastfeeding, most of which are drawn from the recipes in this book. These meals should keep your energy levels up and provide you and your baby with essential nutrients.

breakfast	lunch	dinner	extras
Swiss muesli (p29) yogurt	Bag-baked salmon (pp34–35) with broccoli and rice fruit	Hidden vegetable bolognaise (p127) with spaghetti; My favorite frozen yogurt (p134); fruit	Honey and soy toasted seeds (p29) rice cakes
scrambled eggs on whole-grain toast fruit	Hidden vegetable bolognaise (pp126–127) with spaghetti Fruit fool (pp132–133)	Sweet root soup (pp32–33) tomato and mozzarella salad	Sweet root soup (pp32–33) Chicken and avocado wrap (p37) cottage cheese and fruit
cereal and fruit grilled cheese and tomato on toast	Chicken, broccoli, and snow pea pasta salad (p46) Fruit fool (pp132–133)	lamb chops, baked potato, and grilled tomato Apple and blackberry surprise (pp172–173)	Muffin pizza (pp152–153) vegetables and hummus
oatmeal with honey or fruit yogurt	Pasta with arugula and mascarpone sauce (p41), salad yogurt	grilled tuna with couscous Bananas "Foster" (p131)	Granola bar (p30) fruit
fruit smoothie boiled egg and toast	Southwestern salad (pp44–45) My favorite frozen yogurt (p134); fruit	Sesame beef and broccoli stir-fry (pp38–39) Orchard crisp (p130)	Turkey and tomato sandwich with honey-mustard mayo (p36) dried apricots
half grapefruit whole-grain toast yogurt	Frittata provençale (pp42–43) Orchard crisp (p130)	Sweet root soup (pp32–33) grilled chicken or steak fruit	Southwestern salad (pp44–45) Honey and soy toasted seeds (p29)
Swiss muesli (p29) berries	roast chicken or beef with vegetables fruit ice cream	Frittata provençale (pp42–43), with salad Orchard crisp (p130)	Chinese-style beef wrap (p37) cottage cheese fruit

chapter 2

starting solids: 6–9 months

"My aim is to guide you through weaning and preparing the best first foods for your baby. I'll show you how cooking fresh food for your little one can be easy, and you'll have the added benefit of knowing exactly what has gone into it."

first spoonfuls

Your baby's digestive system will be ready for solids at around six months, and so will her appetite. Weaning can be a daunting time, but it doesn't need to be. I have lots of shortcuts and tips to help you on your way.

The World Health Organization (WHO) guidelines recommend breastfeeding exclusively for the first six months of your baby's life. During this time, in most cases, breast milk or formula provides all the nutrients a baby needs, and should be the only source of nourishment.

● recognizing that she's ready

Don't be in a hurry to wean your baby onto solids. Your baby's digestive and immune systems are not sufficiently developed before she is 17 weeks old (four months), but the WHO now recommends that it's best not to introduce solids until at least 26 weeks of age (six months).

By about six months, your baby will reach a stage when she needs solid foods as well as milk in her diet. For example, the iron stores she inherited from you will have been used up, so it's vital to include iron-rich foods in her diet.

There is, however, no "right" age to introduce solids since every baby is different. If you feel that your baby needs solids earlier than six months,

milk
matters

How much milk does my baby need now that she is on solids?

Babies should have a minimum of 17–21fl oz (500–600ml) of milk each day between 6 and 12 months. You can use cow's milk in cooking and with cereals, but breast or formula milk should be your baby's main drink. If your baby drinks less than 17fl oz (500ml) of formula a day or is breastfed beyond six months, she will need supplementary vitamins A, C, and D up until at least one year. These vitamins are in formula milk, but are lower in breast milk. Part of your baby's intake can be from dairy products such as cheese, yogurt, or milk in cooking. If you're breastfeeding, it's not possible to measure the amount of milk your baby is getting, but her growth and common sense will tell you if she's getting enough.

ask annabel

my top first foods

* **first fruits:** apple, pear, banana, papaya, and avocado

* **first vegetables:** carrot, potato, rutabaga, parsnip, pumpkin, butternut squash, and sweet potato

* **baby rice:** mix baby rice with water, breast, or formula milk, or runny fruit or vegetable purées. Baby rice is easily digested and its milky taste makes an easy transition to solids. Choose one that is sugar-free and enriched with vitamins and iron.

speak to your pediatrician or GP. Many babies are ready for simple purées, like carrot or apple purée, around five months. I think it's important to follow your instincts, because no two babies are the same and mom usually knows best. Here are some signs that your baby is ready to try her first tastes of solid food:

* She is no longer satisfied by a full milk feed.
* She is demanding more frequent milk feeds.
* She is starting to wake up at night, when she was previously sleeping through.
* She is starting to show an interest in the things you eat and seems eager to try them herself.

" Most of the time, you can prepare your baby's food alongside the rest of the family's, and weaning a baby presents a great opportunity to make sure the whole family eats well "

● the best first foods for your baby

The very first foods your baby tries should be easy to digest and unlikely to provoke an allergy (for more information on allergies, see pages 14–16 and for advice on which foods to delay giving to your baby, see page 54). I like to begin with root vegetables such as carrots or sweet potatoes since these have a naturally sweet taste that babies like. Fruits are good for the same reason, but make sure you choose ripe fruits that have a good flavor—it's best to taste them yourself first.

● how to get started

Preparing fresh food for your baby doesn't need to be time-consuming. You can prepare more food than you need and freeze extra individual portions in covered ice cube trays or small plastic containers that are suitable for freezing. By planning ahead with my meal planners (see pages 60–61), you will find that you may need to cook just once or twice a week. Plan your week's shopping and cooking by filling in the blank charts.

Most of the time, you can prepare your baby's food alongside the rest of the family's, and weaning a baby presents a great opportunity to make sure the whole family eats well. If you eat a lot of ready-made meals, it's time to think about making meals from fresh ingredients. If you currently boil vegetables, you may want to think about switching to steaming (see box, right). It's easy to steam vegetables while you prepare your own meal—simply leave out the salt, set aside a portion for your baby, and purée it in a blender when your baby is ready for her meal.

Remember to offer your baby foods that you don't like—your baby might enjoy them even if you don't

Steam vegetables. Broccoli loses over 60 percent of its antioxidants when boiled, but less than 7 percent when steamed

You can prepare meals for your baby without any cooking. Mash or purée a banana, avocado, and papaya

Here are some tips to help you begin weaning:

* **Pick a time of day** when you are not rushed or likely to be distracted. If possible, keep to the same time each day (possibly lunchtime), so that you can begin to establish a routine.

* **At the beginning** it may be a good idea to offer food halfway through a milk feed, so that your baby isn't frantically hungry or too full.

* **To begin with** you need to get your baby used to something other than milk, so it's important to make very runny purées by adding the boiled water from the base of the steamer, or stir in some of your baby's usual milk. As your baby gets used to solids, you can gradually add less liquid.

* **Heat the food thoroughly,** but then let it cool down to room or lukewarm temperature.

* **Use a shallow soft-tipped weaning spoon** to feed your baby. Some babies may not react well to a spoon; if this is the case, you could dip a scrupulously clean finger into the food and let your baby suck the food off it.

* **Feeding your baby** should be a cozy time—you could hold your baby on your lap with your arm around her or sit her facing you in a bouncy chair.

methods of cooking

* **steaming** is by far the best way to preserve the fresh taste and vitamins in vegetables. Vitamins B and C are water soluble and are easily destroyed by overcooking—especially when boiled.

* **baking** potatoes, sweet potatoes, and butternut squash gives them a delicious flavor as it caramelizes their natural sugars. It's easy to bake these at the same time as cooking a meal for the family in the oven.

* **boiling** causes vegetables to lose a lot of their vitamin content in the water, so I don't recommend this method. If you do need to boil vegetables, use the minimum amount of water and add some of the cooking liquid when blending the purée.

* **microwaving** cooks vegetables quickly, requires little water, and doesn't leach out the nutrients into the water, unlike boiling. Some people are concerned that cooking in a microwave isn't good for us, but there is no need to worry. It is a quick, easy, and safe way to cook as long as you follow the manufacturer's instructions.

● portion size

I am often asked how much food a baby should be eating, but the amount that babies eat varies enormously. The amount of food that one baby needs to eat to maintain the same growth rate can be very different than another next baby—even if they are the same age and weight. Babies have different metabolic rates and activity levels, and the foods that you give them can vary in calorie content. For example, a chicken purée will be more filling than a fruit purée. If your baby is growing and seems content, then I would let her be the judge. I recommend feeding a meal until your baby loses interest or until gentle distraction does not regain her interest, and then stopping. Babies are often by nature quite chubby with cute chunky little legs and arms, but these will slim down as your baby becomes more mobile. To be confident that she is receiving all the nutrients she needs, see the chart on pages 12–13.

when can I give my baby ... ?

✳ **gluten**, found in wheat, rye, barley, and oats, can be hard for young babies to digest. Foods containing gluten such as bread or pasta should not be introduced before six months.

✳ **honey** should not be given to babies under 12 months as it can cause infant botulism. Although this is very rare, it is best to be safe, as a baby's digestive system is too immature to cope with the bacteria.

✳ **nuts** For babies with no history of allergy in the family, it is fine to give peanut butter and other finely ground nuts from seven months. However, if there is history of allergy in your family or your baby suffers from eczema, seek medical advice before giving nuts to your baby (for more advice, see pages 15–16). Whole nuts should not be given before the age of five due to the risk of choking.

✳ **milk** Avoid giving cow's milk as a main liquid until your baby is 12 months. However, you can use full-fat cow's milk in cooking and with breakfast cereals from six months. You can give your child semi-skim or skim milk starting around the age of two.

✳ **eggs**, cooked until the white and yolk are solid, can be given to your baby from six months. Do not give raw or undercooked eggs to infants or toddlers.

✳ **fish** Both oily and white fish are great for babies from six months, but don't give more than two portions of oily fish, like salmon or tuna, a week. Shellfish is fine from around nine months.

✳ **cheese** is a nutritious food for your baby from six months. However, you should avoid giving blue cheese and soft unpasteurized cheese, such as Brie, in the first year.

✳ **salt** Babies under one year should not have salt added to their food since this can strain immature kidneys and may cause dehydration. There are other ways to add flavor. See page 65 for advice on this.

✳ **sugar** Unless food is really tart, don't add sugar. Adding sugar is habit-forming and increases the risk of tooth decay.

first vegetable purée

Carrots make excellent weaning food, because babies like their naturally sweet taste. In the first few weeks of weaning, make sure that the carrots are cooked for a long time so that they are soft enough to purée. This method of cooking also works for other root vegetables, such as sweet potatoes, parsnip, and potatoes (cooking times will vary).

- PREPARATION: 5 MINUTES
- COOKING: 15–20 MINUTES STEAMING OR BOILING, OR 9–10 MINUTES MICROWAVING
- MAKES ABOUT 1 CUP
- PROVIDES BETA-CAROTENE
- SUITABLE FOR FREEZING

12oz (340g) carrots, peeled, washed, and chopped or sliced into even-sized pieces

Steam the carrots until tender, 18–20 minutes. Alternatively, put them in a saucepan, cover with boiling water, and cook, covered, for 15–20 minutes.

To microwave, place the carrots in a suitable dish with 3 tbsp water and cover, leaving an air vent. Cook on high for 9–10 minutes, stirring halfway through, then let stand for 1–2 minutes.

Blend the carrots with some of the water from the steamer, the cooking liquid, or a little cooled boiled water (or breast or formula milk), to a very smooth purée. The amount of liquid you add depends on your baby—you may need a little more if your baby finds the purée hard to swallow.

date baby first tried ....

baby's reaction ....

....

....

what I thought ....

....

my variations ....

....

....

....

check reaction

date baby first tried ....

baby's reaction ....
....
....
....
....
....

what I thought ....
....
....

my variations ....
....
....
....
....
....
....
....

check
reaction

butternut squash purée

Butternut squash has a naturally sweet flavor that is popular with babies. This is suitable from six months.

- PREPARATION: 8 MINUTES
- COOKING: 15 MINUTES STEAMING OR BOILING, OR 1½ HOURS IN THE OVEN
- MAKES ABOUT 1¾ CUPS
- PROVIDES BETA-CAROTENE
- SUITABLE FOR FREEZING

1 medium butternut squash, peeled, cut in half lengthwise, and seeds and fibers removed, then cut into cubes

Melted butter, if baking

Steam the squash cubes—or cover them with boiling water—and simmer until tender, about 15 minutes.

Alternatively, to bake, preheat the oven to 400°F (200°C). Cut the squash in half lengthwise and remove the seeds and fibers. Place the halves, cut side up, in a roasting pan, brush with a little melted butter, and cover loosely with foil. Bake until tender, about 1½ hours. Let cool, then scoop out the flesh.

Blend the squash to a purée, then add a little of your baby's usual milk to make a good consistency for your baby.

Variations

Apple and butternut squash purée: Peel, core, and chop 2 apples, and put in a saucepan with 4 tbsp water. Cover and simmer for 5 minutes. Blend to a purée and stir into the butternut squash purée. Makes 2 cups.

Pear and butternut squash purée: Peel, core, and chop 2 ripe pears, and simmer in a small saucepan until soft, 2–3 minutes (juicy pears shouldn't need any extra liquid). Blend to a purée and mix with the butternut squash purée. Makes 2 cups.

annabel karmel

baked sweet potato purée

Baking a sweet potato gives it the best flavor because it caramelizes the natural sugars. Almost any vegetable combined with puréed baked sweet potato will taste delicious (see page 69).

- PREPARATION: 5 MINUTES, PLUS COOLING
- COOKING: 50–60 MINUTES
- MAKES ABOUT 1 CUP
- PROVIDES CALCIUM, BETA-CAROTENE, FOLATE, VIT B_6
- SUITABLE FOR FREEZING

1 medium sweet potato (about 9oz/250g)

½–⅔ cup milk or boiled water

Preheat the oven to 375°F (190°C). Wash and lightly scrub the potato, then pierce it in several places with a skewer, or prick with a fork. Bake the sweet potato until tender, about 50–60 minutes. Let cool.

Cut the potato in half and scoop out the flesh. Blend with enough milk or boiled water to make a smooth purée.

date baby first tried ....

baby's reaction ....
....
....
....
....

what I thought ....
....
....

my variations ....
....
....
....
....
....
....

check
reaction

date baby first tried ....

baby's reaction ....
....
....
....

what I thought ....
....

my variations ....
....
....
....
....
....
....

check reaction

apple and pear purée

Both apples and pears make good first foods for babies, because these fruits are unlikely to cause an allergy. Another benefit of these fruits is that they contain the soluble fiber pectin, which helps little bowels start processing solids efficiently.

- PREPARATION: 5 MINUTES
- COOKING: 6–8 MINUTES
- MAKES ABOUT 1¾ CUPS
- PROVIDES FOLATE, VITS B_2 & C
- SUITABLE FOR FREEZING

2 sweet apples, peeled, cored, and chopped

2 ripe pears, peeled, cored, and chopped

Put the fruit into a heavy-based saucepan with 5 tbsp water. Cover and cook over low heat until tender, 6–8 minutes. Blend to a smooth purée.

Variations: You can also combine fruits and vegetables by making carrot and apple purée or a mixture of sweet potato and pear.

no-cook baby foods

Each of the purées below takes no more than a few minutes to prepare, and makes one serving. You can serve them individually, or mix them. Good combinations are avocado and banana; avocado, banana, and yogurt; and papaya and banana.

avocado

Avocados offer the perfect ratio of good fat (monounsaturated), protein, and carbohydrate, all in one food. Being nutrient-dense, they'll help fuel your baby's rapid growth in the first year. Avocado provides folate and vitamins A and B_3.

Cut ½ small, ripe avocado in half, remove the pit, and scoop out the flesh. Mash this with a little of your baby's usual milk until smooth.

banana

Because bananas are easily portable, they are ideal to take with you when you are out and about and want to feed your baby. Bananas provide potassium, magnesium, selenium, and folate.

Peel ½ small, ripe banana and mash with a fork until smooth. To begin with, you may want to mix the mashed banana with a little of your baby's usual milk to thin down the consistency.

papaya

Papaya provides beta-carotene, folate, and vitamins B_3, C, and E, and it contains an enzyme that aids digestion.

Cut ½ small, ripe papaya in half and remove the black seeds and peel. Mash the flesh until very smooth. Alternatively, if the papaya flesh is fibrous, purée in a blender.

---

date baby first tried ....

baby's reaction ....
....
....
....

what I thought ....
....
....

my variations ....
....
....
....
....
....
....
....

check reaction

meal planner: first spoonfuls

The meal planner below provides suggestions for your baby's first meals. Use the spaces to record what your baby eats along with her milk feeds. On the opposite page, map out your baby's first tastes and record what she eats and drinks.

WEEK 1	first taste	my baby's feeds
day 1	First vegetable purée (p55)	
day 2	Baked sweet potato purée (p57)	
day 3	Apple and pear purée (p58)	
day 4	Banana (p59)	
day 5	First vegetable purée (p55) or Baked sweet potato purée (p57)	
day 6	Butternut squash purée (p56)	
day 7	baby cereal Banana (p59)	

● feeding solids

Simple fruit and vegetable pureés are perfect for your baby's first meals. In the early days, you'll need to feed your baby just one meal a day, but this can increase to two by week three.

WEEK 2	first taste	my baby's feeds
day 1		
day 2		
day 3		
day 4		
day 5		
day 6		
day 7		

meal planner: weeks 3 and 4

Use these pages to record the meals and milk feeds you give to your baby over the next weeks. I've provided some suggestions for when you move on to two meals a day. If you want to record your baby's first tastes for longer, simply photocopy these pages.

WEEK 3	breakfast	lunch	my baby's feeds
day 1	pear purée and baby rice	First vegetable purée (p55)	
day 2	apple purée	Butternut squash purée (p56)	
day 3	baby cereal Banana (p59)	carrot and parsnip purée	
day 4	Avocado and Banana (p59)	Apple and butternut squash purée (p56)	
day 5	Papaya (p59) baby cereal	Baked sweet potato purée (p57)	
day 6	Apple and pear purée (p58)	Avocado (p59)	
day 7	baby cereal Banana (p59)	carrot or parsnip and apple purée	

● food allergies

If your baby is at risk of allergies (see pages 14–16), introduce low-allergen foods at first, such as apples, pears, and root vegetables, and try new foods one at a time over 2–3 consecutive days.

WEEK 4	breakfast	lunch	my baby's feeds
day 1			
day 2			
day 3			
day 4			
day 5			
day 6			
day 7			

other favorites

Use this page to write down your other favorite recipes, ideas for combinations of different fruits and vegetables, or recipe recommendations from your friends and family. Remember to introduce your baby to new foods one at a time. Enjoy experimenting!

new tastes

Once your baby is comfortable with the simple purées, you can begin to introduce more flavors. With your guidance, your baby will be excited to discover that foods have different tastes and new textures.

The needs of babies and toddlers are different than those of adults. Low-fat, high-fiber diets are great for adults, but not appropriate for babies or young children who need more fat and concentrated sources of calories and nutrients to fuel their rapid growth. Babies shouldn't be given too much fiber since it tends to be bulky and can fill them up before they get all the nutrients they need for proper growth and development. Excess fiber can hinder the absorption of vital nutrients and can cause other problems such as diarrhea.

Babies should continue to eat a wide variety of fruits and vegetables. However, after the first few weeks of weaning, you can begin to offer your baby foods that are higher in calories such as mashed avocado, fruit mixed with Greek yogurt, or vegetables in a cheese sauce.

● fruit

At six months, your baby should be able to eat most fruits. However, there are a few fruits that can give babies upset tummies or cause a reaction. To begin with, it is best to give only small amounts of citrus fruits (such as oranges), berries (such as strawberries), and kiwi fruits to your baby, because they can cause redness around the mouth, especially in babies and children with eczema. This is an irritant effect, and rarely due to

experiment with flavors

✳ **combine ingredients** to make interesting flavors. Don't be afraid to mix sweet with savory. Fruit with puréed chicken or fish, for example, is a favorite with many babies. Try feeding your baby lots of different combinations.

✳ **add garlic**. Since you can't add salt to babies' food before one year, I like to use garlic to add flavor instead. Garlic is very healthy—in fact, the Greeks and Romans ate it before going to war because they believed it made them strong. Allicin,

which gives off the strong smell, helps to kill off nasty bacteria and viruses. Eaten regularly, garlic can help to prevent colds.

✳ **herbs**, like fresh thyme and basil, are another great way to add flavor without adding salt.

allergy. Dried fruits are fine in moderation, but be careful, because too many can have a laxative effect. Choose dried apricots that are not treated with sulphur dioxide (E220)—this is used to preserve their bright orange color and can trigger an asthma attack in susceptible babies.

vegetables

At six months, your baby can eat all vegetables, but stronger tasting vegetables such as spinach are best mixed with root vegetables like sweet potatoes. It is absolutely fine to use frozen peas or spinach when making baby food—vegetables are frozen within hours of being picked, thus sealing in all the nutrients. Frozen vegetables can be more nutritious than fresh.

breads and cereals

From six months, your baby can have gluten, so you can ditch the baby rice and give cereals like soaked muesli and oatmeal. You can also offer rice cakes, toast, pita bread, or halved bagels to your baby from around eight months.

dairy

Although you should wait until your baby is at least 12 months to introduce cow's milk as a drink, it can be used with cereal and in cooking from six months. Yogurt is popular, but choose the full-fat rather than low-fat variety, and check the label because it can often be high in sugar.

It is good to add cheese to vegetables or fish since it's rich in calcium and protein, and provides the calories that babies need for their rapid growth. Cheddar, Parmesan, ricotta, and cream cheese are all great choices.

meat

Iron is very important for your baby's mental and physical development. A baby is born with a store

---

drink dilemma

Should I give my baby juice or water to drink as well as milk?

Water is the best drink for babies under 12 months. If your baby is less than six months, boil tap water and let it cool before giving it to him. Bottled mineral water is unsuitable for young babies since it contains high levels of mineral salts. If your baby is on a vegetarian diet, then it's a good idea to give a vitamin C-rich fruit juice with meals, as this helps him to absorb iron from his food. All babies can have a little unsweetened juice, but dilute it with at least three parts water to one part juice. Too much juice can cause diarrhea. Drinks with added sugar or artificial sweeteners are unsuitable. It's best to give juice in a cup and put only milk or water in his bottle. Introduce a two-handled sippy cup as soon as he's ready to hold one.

ask annabel

tips

Remember to check the labels. Baby rusks and yogurts can be high in sugar

Cooking fish in a microwave is a great option when you're pressed for time; it takes just a few minutes to cook

Avoid blue cheese before 12 months since the strong molds can upset little tummies

of iron that lasts for about six months. After this, it is important that your baby obtains the iron he needs from his diet. Iron in foods of animal origin such as red meat or poultry is much better absorbed than iron in foods of plant origin like green vegetables or cereal. Pork and lamb are lower in iron than beef, and liver is the best source of iron. When giving babies chicken, choose the brown meat as well as the breast meat since it contains twice as much iron and zinc as the white. Good non-meat sources of iron include legumes, fortified whole-grain cereals, and leafy green vegetables.

fish

It is hard to find jars of purée containing fish, which is why making fish dishes for your baby is especially important. Fish is an excellent food for babies and combines well with a cheese sauce. Oily fish, such as salmon, trout, fresh tuna, and sardines, is rich in essential fatty acids (EFAs), and I can't stress enough how important these are for the development of your baby's brain, vision, and nervous system. Ideally, you should give your baby oily fish twice a week, but no more, as there are concerns over the build-up of toxins in the body. Alternative sources of EFAs for babies on vegetarian diets are soybean products.

It's important not to overcook fish. Also, check the fish carefully with clean fingers to make sure that there are no bones.

eggs

Eggs are very nutritious and fine for your baby to eat from six months as long as the white and yolk are cooked until solid. Eggs from chickens that have been fed an omega-3-rich diet are also another great source of EFAs. If there is history of allergy in the family or your baby suffers from eczema, your baby is more likely to suffer from an egg allergy. Consult your doctor if you're concerned.

baby's likes and dislikes

Don't be surprised if your baby shows taste preferences at this early age. Babies have well-developed taste buds and have likes and dislikes just like adults. Every baby is different. If he rejects a food, try serving it again in a few weeks—he may have changed his mind.

If your baby does have a particular favorite, it's best not to offer it all the time. Introducing a wide variety of tastes, colors, and textures is especially important in your baby's first year so he learns to accept a variety of foods and does not become fixed in his food preferences.

date baby first tried ....

baby's reaction ....

....

....

....

....

what I thought ....

....

....

my variations ....

....

....

....

....

....

....

check reaction

tasty vegetable trio

Nutritionists and scientists agree that broccoli is truly a miraculous vegetable—a powerhouse of antioxidants. The best way to cook it is by lightly steaming it, or microwaving it in very little water, because when boiled it can lose more than 50 percent of its vitamin C content.

- PREPARATION: 10 MINUTES
- COOKING: 20 MINUTES
- MAKES ABOUT 2 CUPS
- PROVIDES PROTEIN, CALCIUM, FOLATE, BETA-CAROTENE, VITS B_{12}, C, & D
- SUITABLE FOR FREEZING

3 medium carrots (about 7oz/200g), peeled and sliced

½ cup broccoli florets

2 tbsp butter

2 medium, ripe tomatoes, peeled, seeded, and cut into pieces (about 1 cup)

½ cup shredded Cheddar cheese

Steam the carrots for 10 minutes, then add the broccoli (ideally use a two-tiered steamer) and continue to steam until tender, about 7 minutes.

Melt the butter in a pan and sauté the tomatoes for 2–3 minutes. Remove from the heat and stir in the cheese until melted. Add the steamed carrots and broccoli and blend to a purée in the pan using an immersion blender, adding a little of the steaming liquid for a runnier consistency.

Variation: Use cauliflower instead of broccoli.

sweet potato and spinach purée

A good way to introduce stronger-tasting green vegetables to your baby is to mix them with root vegetables. A baked sweet potato is particularly good as a base, because baking this vegetable accentuates its sweetness. It's worth popping some extra sweet potatoes into the oven when you are making a roast for the rest of the family.

- PREPARATION: 6 MINUTES, PLUS COOLING
- COOKING: ABOUT 55 MINUTES
- MAKES ABOUT 1¼ CUPS
- PROVIDES CALCIUM, BETA-CAROTENE, VITS A, C, & D
- SUITABLE FOR FREEZING

½ cup fresh baby spinach leaves, carefully washed

1 tbsp butter

1 sweet potato (about 9oz/250g), baked and cooled (see page 57)

½ cup milk

Put the washed spinach into a pan and cook until wilted, about 3 minutes. Remove the spinach from the pan and press out any excess liquid. Melt the butter in the pan and sauté the spinach for 1 minute.

Halve the baked sweet potato and scoop out the flesh, then blend to a purée with the sautéed spinach and milk.

date baby first tried ....

baby's reaction ....
....
....
....
....

what I thought ....
....
....
....

my variations ....
....
....
....
....
....

check
reaction

date baby first tried.....................................

baby's reaction...
....
....
....
....

what I thought..
....
....

my variations...
....
....
....
....
....
....
....

check
reaction

oatmeal with apple, pear, and apricot

This makes a nutritious breakfast and is suitable from six months. Pack up portions of the fruit purée and freeze. Then you can thaw them overnight, ready to mix with your baby's cereal in the morning. As your baby gets older, you can simply stir in rather than purée.

- PREPARATION: 8 MINUTES
- COOKING: 8 MINUTES
- MAKES ABOUT 1¾ CUPS FRUIT PURÉE
  (2–3 TBSP PER PORTION OF OATMEAL)
- PROVIDES CALCIUM, IRON, FOLATE, BETA-CAROTENE, VIT C
- FRUIT PURÉE SUITABLE FOR FREEZING

1 apple, peeled, cored, and chopped

1 ripe pear, peeled, cored, and chopped

4 ready-to-eat dried apricots, chopped

To serve (per portion)

6 tbsp milk

1 heaping tbsp instant oatmeal or quick-cook rolled oats

Put the fruit into a saucepan with 4 tbsp water. Cover and cook until tender, about 6 minutes. Let cool, then blend to a purée.

To make the oatmeal, combine the milk and oats in another small saucepan. Bring to a boil, then simmer, stirring occasionally, for about 3 minutes. Combine the fruit and the oatmeal, and blend to a purée.

my first beef casserole

I like to introduce red meat to babies soon after six months, because their store of iron inherited from their mother runs out at around this age, and red meat provides the richest source of iron. The best way to prepare red meat for babies is to cook it slowly with root vegetables.

- PREPARATION: 10 MINUTES
- COOKING: 1 HOUR
- MAKES ABOUT 2½ CUPS
- PROVIDES PROTEIN, IRON, POTASSIUM, SELENIUM, ZINC, BETA-CAROTENE, PREBIOTICS
- SUITABLE FOR FREEZING

1 tbsp olive oil

1 small red onion, chopped

1 clove garlic, crushed

¼ tsp fresh thyme leaves or a pinch of dried thyme

4oz (115g) lean chuck steak, cut into small chunks

2 tsp tomato paste

I large sweet potato (about 8oz/225g), peeled and chopped

2 potatoes (about 10oz/300g), peeled and chopped

1 cup chicken stock

Heat the oil in a Dutch oven and sauté the onion over low heat until soft, about 5 minutes. (Alternatively, you can use a heavy-bottomed stock pot with a tight-fitting lid.) Add the garlic and thyme, and cook for 1 minute longer. Add the chuck steak and sauté for a few minutes until seared. Add the tomato paste and sauté for 1 minute, stirring.

Add the sweet potato and potatoes, and pour in the chicken stock. Bring to a boil, then cover and simmer, stirring occasionally, until the meat is very tender, about 50 minutes. You may need to add a little extra stock during cooking. Let cool slightly, then blend to a purée.

> Often it's the texture rather than the taste of red meat that babies object to. Mixing beef with root vegetables and cooking it slowly gives it a soft texture that babies like

date baby first tried ....

baby's reaction ....
....
....
....

what I thought ....
....
....

my variations ....
....
....
....
....
....
....
....

check reaction

my favorite chicken purée

This is very tasty and a good introduction to chicken. Adding a little sweetness by combining the chicken with sweet potato and dried apricots makes it appealing to babies. I've used chicken thigh here, because it has a softer, more moist consistency than breast, and the dark meat of chicken has twice as much iron and zinc than the white.

- PREPARATION: 10 MINUTES
- COOKING: 25 MINUTES
- MAKES ABOUT 2½ CUPS
- PROVIDES PROTEIN, IRON, SELENIUM, ZINC, BETA-CAROTENE, VIT C
- SUITABLE FOR FREEZING

2 chicken thighs

1 tbsp olive oil

½ cup sliced leek

2 cups peeled and chopped sweet potato

⅓ cup dried apricots, halved

⅔ cup tomato purée

Scant 1 cup chicken stock or water

Remove the meat from the chicken thighs and discard the skin and fat. I use about 4oz (115g) of chicken thigh meat for this recipe. Cut into chunks.

Heat the oil in a pan and sauté the leek until softened, about 4 minutes. Add the chicken and sauté until the chunks are white on all sides, about 2 minutes. Add the sweet potato and sauté for 1 minute. Stir in the dried apricots, tomato purée, and chicken stock. Bring to a boil, then cover and simmer for about 15 minutes. Blend to a purée.

potato and carrot mash with salmon

It's hard to find jars of baby purée with oily fish like salmon, which is the best source of essential fatty acids that are vital for your baby's brain and visual development. A mashed potato and carrot mixed with a little milk, butter, and cheese makes a good base for a baby's meal. I prefer to mash the potato by hand, because puréeing it in a blender breaks down the natural starches, leaving a gooey texture. If mashed food is too lumpy for your baby, you could try using a baby food grinder or potato ricer to prepare this.

- PREPARATION: 10 MINUTES
- COOKING: 20 MINUTES
- MAKES ABOUT 1¾ CUPS
- PROVIDES PROTEIN, OMEGA-3s, CALCIUM, IRON, SELENIUM, BETA-CAROTENE, VITS A & D
- SUITABLE FOR FREEZING

2 cups peeled and chopped potatoes

1 cup peeled and sliced carrots

3½ tbsp milk

1 tbsp butter

⅓ cup shredded Cheddar cheese

3½–4oz (90–115g) salmon fillet, skinned

Put the potatoes and carrot into a saucepan, cover with boiling water, and cook until the vegetables are tender, about 20 minutes. Drain and mash together with 3 tbsp milk, the butter, and cheese.

While the vegetables are cooking, put the salmon into a suitable microwave dish with the remaining ½ tbsp milk, and microwave on high for 1½ minutes. (If you don't have a microwave, you can steam the fish over the vegetables for 5–6 minutes.) Flake the fish, checking to make sure that there are no bones in it.

Mix the fish into the potato and carrot mash.

date baby first tried ....

baby's reaction ....

what I thought ....

my variations ....

check reaction

fillet of fish with cheesy vegetable sauce

This dish makes a good introduction to fish for your baby. Sole is one of the best fish to start with due to its lovely moist, soft texture. I like to boost the nutrients in the cheese sauce by adding steamed carrots and broccoli, which are rich in vitamins. If you don't have a microwave, you can poach the fish in a small saucepan of milk instead.

- PREPARATION: 8 MINUTES
- COOKING: 15 MINUTES
- MAKES ABOUT 1½ CUPS
- PROVIDES PROTEIN, CALCIUM, IRON, SELENIUM, BETA-CAROTENE, VITS A, B$_{12}$, C, & D
- SUITABLE FOR FREEZING

1 medium carrot, peeled and sliced

½ cup broccoli florets

1 small sole fillet (or similar white fish fillet), skinned (about 3½oz/90g)

1 tbsp butter

Sauce

1 tbsp butter

1 tbsp all-purpose flour

⅔ cup milk

6 tbsp shredded Cheddar cheese

Steam the carrots for 5 minutes, then add the broccoli florets and continue to steam until the vegetables are tender, about 7 minutes longer. Meanwhile, put the fish fillet into a suitable microwave dish, dot with butter, and microwave on high for about 1½ minutes.

To make the cheese sauce, melt the butter, stir in the flour, and cook over low heat for 1 minute. Gradually whisk in the milk. Bring to a boil and simmer for a few minutes until thickened and smooth. Remove from the heat and stir in the cheese until melted.

Blend the vegetables and flaked fish with the cheese sauce to a purée.

Note: As your baby gets older, you can mash the vegetables and fish with the sauce, rather than making a purée.

meal planner: new tastes

This meal planner provides suggestions for your baby's meals, many of which are drawn from this book. Either use the planner pages to map out your baby's meals for the next weeks or to keep a record of your baby's diet week-by-week.

breakfast	lunch	dinner	extras
Oatmeal with apple, pear, and apricot (p70)	My favorite chicken purée (p72)	First vegetable purée (p55) or Baked sweet potato purée (p57)	After the savory purée at lunch and dinner, you can give your baby a fruit purée or yogurt. Introduce new foods such as mango, peach, and cantaloupe—these don't need to be cooked and can be served alone or with baby rice or a banana.
apple or mango purée and cereal	My favorite chicken purée (p72)	Tasty vegetable trio (p68)	
Banana (p59) or mashed peach and banana cereal	Fillet of fish with cheesy vegetable sauce (pp74–75)	Tasty vegetable trio (p68)	
Oatmeal with apple, pear, and apricot (p70) yogurt	Fillet of fish with cheesy vegetable sauce (pp74–75)	Sweet potato and spinach purée (p69)	
pear purée and baby rice yogurt	My first beef casserole (p71)	Sweet potato and spinach purée (p69)	
Avocado and banana (p59) cereal	My first beef casserole (p71)	Butternut squash purée (p56)	
Apple and pear purée (p58) cereal	Potato and carrot mash with salmon (p73)	My favorite chicken purée (p72)	

● a varied diet

Even at this young age, your baby doesn't
need to eat the same things every day. Vary
breakfasts with different fruit purées and
serve with oatmeal, cereal, or baby rice.

WEEK 1	breakfast	lunch	dinner	extras
day 1				
day 2				
day 3				
day 4				
day 5				
day 6				
day 7				

meal planner: weeks 2 and 3

Use these planners to record the meals you give your baby over the following weeks. If you want to record your baby's meals for longer than three weeks, simply photocopy this page. Keep note of your baby's milk feeds too, if you wish.

WEEK 2	breakfast	lunch	dinner	extras
day 1				
day 2				
day 3				
day 4				
day 5				
day 6				
day 7				

● experiment with flavors

Try making different combinations of first foods for your baby, such as apple and pear (p58) or carrot and parsnip. Mix fruits and vegetables too, such as apple and butternut squash (p56).

WEEK 3	breakfast	lunch	dinner	extras
day 1				
day 2				
day 3				
day 4				
day 5				
day 6				
day 7				

other favorites

Use this page to write down your other favorite recipes, ideas for combinations of different fruits and vegetables, or recipe recommendations from your friends and family. Remember to introduce your baby to new foods one at a time. Enjoy experimenting!

older babies: 9–12 months

"Your child is changing from a baby to a mini person and it's no surprise that he'll soon prefer to feed himself. Finger foods are popular, and I've provided you with tasty and nutritious recipes that are perfect for little fingers."

fingers and spoons

Toward the end of the first year, a baby's weight gain tends to slow down dramatically. This is a time of growing independence, and often babies who have been good eaters in the past become more difficult to feed.

By around nine months, you'll notice that your baby may prefer to feed himself. He'll probably let you know that he's ready by grabbing the spoon you're feeding him with or snatching food off your plate. By doing this, your baby learns about food's texture, smell, and flavor, so it's important to give him an assortment of foods to try.

textures

You begin to think everything is going swimmingly with your baby slurping his way through your puréed carrots and sweet potatoes; then you ditch the blender and it all goes downhill. The transition from perfectly puréed to lumpy food can be difficult since many babies are lazy about chewing, but it's important to give your baby grated, mashed, and chopped food. The muscles a baby uses to chew are the same ones used for speech, so encouraging your baby to chew will help his speech development too.

I would recommend stirring tiny soft lumps, like pasta stars or mini pasta shells, into your baby's favorite purées, gradually increasing the texture and lumpiness of his food. Couscous is another good food; it's a form of grain made from wheat and you can find it in most supermarkets

next to the rice. It's quick to prepare and nice and soft, so it acts as a gradual transition from purées to a more lumpy texture, and it is tasty with diced vegetables or chicken.

finger foods

This can be a stressful time for parents, since babies find it hard to cope with more lumpy food and generally prefer to feed themselves than be fed. Interestingly, while many babies refuse anything with lumps in it, they will often happily

chew on finger foods such as cucumber sticks or pieces of fruit. Around eight or nine months, as your child's hand to eye coordination matures, finger foods will become an increasingly important part of his diet. Your baby's aim will be far from perfect, but the more you allow him to experiment, the quicker he will learn to feed himself.

● savory finger foods

To begin with, it's best to give steamed vegetables rather than raw. Your baby may be able to bite off a piece of raw carrot and then be unable to chew, so there is a risk of choking. Try steamed carrot sticks or broccoli florets. Later on your baby will become more proficient at chewing, and you can give him raw vegetables. Many babies prefer to be given a whole carrot or chunk of cucumber to chew on, rather than chopping them into small pieces. Other ideas include rice cakes, bread sticks, and pieces of avocado.

● fruity finger foods

Fresh fruit makes perfect finger food, but do be careful not to give fruits with pits or whole grapes, since these may cause your baby to choke. Try cutting up a selection of fruits, lay them out on a tray, and let your child pick them up and dunk them into a tasty dip. Begin with soft fruits like bananas, pears, or peaches. Cantaloupe wedges, peeled pear or apple slices, or grapes cut in half are also good. Try dried apricots too—they are a great source of fiber, iron, and vitamins.

● something cool for sore gums

During the three months up to your baby's first birthday, he may cut several teeth, and sore gums may make eating unpleasant. It's a good idea to pop something cool like cucumber sticks in the fridge since chewing on something cold can be very soothing. Or freeze a banana for 20 minutes, peel it, and let your baby suck on it.

mealtime mayhem

I'm worried that my baby will never have good table manners—she throws food everywhere. What can I do?

This is an age when children experiment with their food, and if you are the type of person who likes everything neat and tidy, you are going to have to take a deep breath since your child is going to want to play with her food. She's going to want to touch, hold, and occasionally drop her food. The more you allow her to experiment, the quicker she'll learn to feed herself. Allow her to explore the feel of food and take time eating it. It may be messy, but you should not discourage her attempts or worry about her table manners. She will pick up on your anxieties and mealtimes will turn into a battleground. See opposite page for tips on dealing with the mess.

ask annabel

Your baby's hands should always be washed before and after eating

Put a little petroleum jelly around your baby's mouth and chin if he dribbles while teething to prevent any soreness

As your baby starts to crawl, he will need more energy-rich foods, such as meat, chicken, cheese, pasta, and dried fruit

You could also try making your own healthy fresh fruit popsicles. You can purée fruits like peaches or mangoes and mix them with orange or tropical fruit juice, or purée, and sieve berry fruits, such as strawberries or raspberries, and mix them with strawberry yogurt. Alternatively, simply pour fresh fruit juice or a smoothie into a popsicle mold and freeze. See pages 135–137 recipes for popsicles and smoothie sticks.

Other good foods for babies during teething include yogurt, fruit purées, jelly, and risotto.

mini meals

Babies have small stomachs and cannot take in too much at each mealtime, so they need light meals that are full of protein and slow-releasing carbohydrates. There are some great finger foods that supply everything they need. Try the delicious Salmon fishcakes (pages 98–99), Poached chicken balls (page 101), and Fish goujons (page 115). A favorite with my children is the Tuna tortilla melt (page 119).

encouraging healthy eating

At this age, children are fascinated by what older children and adults are doing, so it is important that your baby is surrounded by people eating

normal, healthy meals. Try to sit alongside your baby and eat your own lunch while you feed him. Invite another mom and baby around occasionally—especially if the baby is a good eater.

dealing with mess

Mealtimes are going to get messy, so it's a good idea to put a large plastic or mess mat under the highchair to catch the food that falls on the floor. Other useful pieces of equipment include a spoon and fork set that is attached to the highchair tray or to the table with a curly wire—so that even if your baby flings the cutlery down, it doesn't drop on the floor. A bowl with a strong suction base is also a great purchase.

There is no need to be obsessive about germs. It's fine to use an antibacterial wipe to clean your baby's highchair but, remember, your baby picks things up from the floor and puts them in his mouth all the time.

One very common thing that pediatric dietitians talk about is children who are afraid of mess. This seems to be at the root of many toddler eating problems. Allow your baby to experiment—he's bound to get himself into a mess, but it's not a good idea to continually wipe your child's face clean when he is eating.

● choking

Usually, babies gag, cough, or spit food out if they cannot swallow it. However, you should always stay with your baby when he's feeding himself in case he chokes. Just because your child can chew off a piece of food, like a piece of toast, it doesn't mean that he can chew it properly. Sometimes babies chew off pieces of food and then store them in their mouths, so always check when you lift your child out of the highchair that there is no lumpy food left in his mouth. When my children were babies, I sometimes found that they would keep food in their mouths long after I thought they had finished. Check that your baby has swallowed everything before you leave the room—especially if you are just starting him on hard finger foods.

* **If your child chokes,** don't try to retrieve the food with your fingers, since this can push it further down the windpipe.

* **Lay your baby face down** on your forearm, with his head lower than his body. Give him five sharp pats across the top of his back between his shoulder blades. Pick out any visible obstructions with your forefinger and thumb.

* **If the obstruction is still present,** turn your baby over on to his back and give five sharp thrusts, pushing down with two fingers in the middle of his chest, at a rate of one every three seconds. Then check your baby's mouth again for any obstruction.

* **If unsuccessful, repeat the sequence** and call emergency services immediately.

finger food ideas

* **vegetables**, such as broccoli, carrots, cauliflower, parsnip, and asparagus. Lightly steam or boil them at first so they are a little crunchy, but not hard. Once your baby is more proficient at chewing, you can give him raw vegetables. Other tasty ideas include halved cherry tomatoes and slices of avocado.

* **fruit** such as banana chunks, apple, peach, melon, or pear slices. Soft fruits are best at first if your baby finds it difficult to chew. Serve with a tasty dip.

* **dried fruit** like apricots, figs, prunes, or large pieces of apple. Be careful with smaller pieces, such as raisins, since they could cause your baby to choke.

* **mini sandwiches** with soft fillings (see pages 90–92).

* **starchy finger foods** such as strips of toast or pita bread, mini rice cakes, rusks, or bread sticks.

* **dry cereals** are very handy when you're on the go. Avoid the sugar-coated varieties, though.

* **cold, cooked pasta shapes** are great energy-boosters.

* **cheese cut into sticks, or cheese slices or mini cheeses.**

* **protein-rich finger foods** such as chicken balls (see page 101 for recipe) or salmon fishcakes (see page 99), or small pieces of cooked chicken or turkey.

* **popsicles and smoothie sticks,** (see pages 135–137 for recipes), and jello and yogurt can soothe teething gums.

finger foods my baby has tried

Finger foods encourage self-feeding and give your baby a sense of independence. Try to include some finger foods at each meal. See the ideas on the opposite page and record which ones your baby has tried and enjoyed and which ones he disliked.

date baby first tried ....

baby's reaction ....

....

....

....

what I thought ....

....

....

my variations ....

....

....

....

....

....

check
reaction

my first muesli

Baby oatmeal is nice and fine, so it makes a good base on which to add extra—and new—textures.

● PREPARATION: 4–5 MINUTES
● COOKING: NONE
● MAKES 1 PORTION
● PROVIDES POTASSIUM, CALCIUM, VITS A, B_1, B_3 & D, PREBIOTICS

2 tbsp baby oatmeal

2 tbsp milk (or breast milk or formula)

1 tbsp strawberry or vanilla yogurt

½ small banana, mashed or diced

Mix the oatmeal, milk, and yogurt together, then stir in the banana. Add a little extra milk if your baby likes a runnier consistency.

french toast fingers

Cinnamon raisin bread makes a nice alternative to ordinary white bread for French toast—it reminds me of bread pudding. If you don't have any handy, then you can simply add a large pinch of cinnamon to the egg mixture and serve the French toast with a few raisins. Flattening the bread makes it easier for small mouths to chew.

- PREPARATION: 5 MINUTES
- COOKING: 4–5 MINUTES
- MAKES 1 PORTION
- PROVIDES IRON, SELENIUM, VITS D & E

1 small slice cinnamon raisin bread
1 egg yolk
1 tsp heavy cream (or milk)
1–2 drops of pure vanilla extract
Pinch of sugar
1 tbsp butter

Flatten the bread by rolling it out with a rolling pin until it is about half of its original thickness. Beat the egg yolk, cream, vanilla, and sugar together in a small, flat dish.

Melt the butter in a frying pan over medium heat. When the butter is foaming, dip the bread into the egg mixture, then fry in the hot butter for about 2 minutes on each side until golden. Let cool until warm, then serve cut into fingers.

Note: To make two portions, use a whole egg and double everything else.

" You can also make French toast using white bread or challah (Jewish egg bread). Slices of grilled cheese on toast make a delicious breakfast for older babies too "

date baby first tried ....

baby's reaction ....

what I thought ....

my variations ....

check reaction

finger food sandwiches

The trick to good sandwiches is to not have too much bread or too much filling. I like to flatten the bread by rolling with a rolling pin so that the sandwich is easier for small children to eat. For toddlers, it is best to cut the sandwich into bite-size pieces, but as your child gets older it can be fun to cut the sandwiches into fingers or other shapes.

tasty tuna

I find that tuna packed in olive oil has a slightly nicer flavor, but you can use tuna packed in water if you prefer. Older children may like ½ tbsp drained canned corn added to the mix.

- PREPARATION: 8 MINUTES
- COOKING: NONE
- MAKES 1–2 PORTIONS
- PROVIDES PROTEIN, IRON, ZINC

¼ cup drained canned tuna

1 tbsp mayonnaise

1 tsp ketchup

Salt and pepper

2 slices bread, flattened

Put the tuna in a bowl and mash it well, then stir in the mayonnaise and ketchup. Season to taste with salt and pepper. Spread on one slice of bread and cover with the other slice. Cut the sandwich into squares or fingers.

cream cheese and jam

I like raspberry jam because it has no lumps, which toddlers tend to prefer. However, you can use your favorite jam, jelly, or marmalade.

- PREPARATION: 5 MINUTES
- COOKING: NONE
- MAKES 1–2 PORTIONS
- PROVIDES PROTEIN, CALCIUM, VIT D

2 tbsp cream cheese, at room temperature

2 slices bread, flattened

1½ tsp raspberry jam

Spread 1 tbsp of cream cheese over each slice of bread. Spread the jam on top of one slice and cover with the remaining slice. Cut the sandwich into squares or fingers.

---

date baby first tried ....

baby's reaction ....

what I thought ....

my variations ....

check reaction

date baby first tried ....

baby's reaction ....

what I thought ....

my variations ....

check reaction

double cheese sandwich

These are also nice as open-faced sandwiches—just use shredded or sliced Cheddar cheese and only half of the cream cheese base.

● PREPARATION: 8 MINUTES
● COOKING: NONE
● MAKES 1–2 PORTIONS
● PROVIDES PROTEIN, CALCIUM, VIT D

2 tbsp cream cheese

1½ tsp ketchup

2 slices bread, flattened

¼ cup shredded or thinly sliced cheddar cheese

Mix the cream cheese and ketchup together in a small bowl. Spread half over each slice of bread. Top one slice with the cheese and cover with the remaining slice. Cut the sandwich into squares or fingers.

cream cheese and banana sandwich

This is also nice spread on toast for breakfast.

● PREPARATION: 5 MINUTES
● COOKING: NONE
● MAKES 1–2 PORTIONS
● PROVIDES PROTEIN, POTASSIUM, CALCIUM, VIT D

2 tbsp cream cheese

1 tsp maple syrup (or clear honey for babies over one year)

½ small banana, mashed

2 slices bread, flattened

Mix the cream cheese and maple syrup (or honey) together in a bowl, then stir in the banana. Spread over one slice of bread and top with the remaining slice. Cut the sandwich into squares or fingers.

broccoli and cheese baby bites

This is essentially a broccoli and cheese purée bound with fresh bread crumbs. It makes a good finger food when rolled into small balls and coated in crumbs and fried—many babies at this age refuse to be fed with a spoon. You must chill the balls well before cooking.

- PREPARATION: 30 MINUTES, PLUS AT LEAST 1 HOUR CHILLING
- COOKING: 2–3 MINUTES PER BATCH
- MAKES ABOUT 20 (3–4 PER PORTION)
- PROVIDES PROTEIN, CALCIUM, FOLATE, VITS A, C &, D
- SUITABLE FOR FREEZING

1 heaping cup broccoli florets

4 slices white bread, crusts removed

¼ cup shredded sharp Cheddar cheese

¼ cup shredded mozzarella cheese

1–2 eggs, beaten

3 tbsp dry bread crumbs

3 tbsp freshly grated Parmesan cheese

1 tbsp all-purpose flour

3–4 tbsp sunflower oil, for frying

Steam the broccoli florets until soft, 7–8 minutes. Transfer them to a plate and set aside to cool.

Put the bread in a food processor and process to crumbs, then pour into a bowl. Put the broccoli, Cheddar, and mozzarella in the food processor and purée until smooth. Add to the bread crumbs and squish everything together until well-combined. (The mixture may need a little liquid to help it bind, in which case add 1–2 tsp of the beaten egg.)

Mix the dry bread crumbs and Parmesan on a large plate. Put the flour on another plate and the beaten egg in a bowl. Roll teaspoonfuls of the broccoli mixture into small balls. Dust with flour, then dip in the egg and, finally, roll in the bread crumbs. Let set in the refrigerator for at least 1 hour or, preferably, overnight.

Heat the oil in a nonstick frying pan and cook the balls over high heat, turning frequently, until golden brown all over, 2–3 minutes. Drain on paper towels and let cool to warm before serving.

Note: The bites can be kept in the refrigerator for 2–3 days and then cooked when needed. To freeze, individually freeze, then transfer to plastic bags; cook from frozen, adding an extra minute to the cooking time.

date baby first tried.....................

baby's reaction.....................

what I thought.....................

my variations.....................

check reaction

"Broccoli is king of the superstar vegetables. It is one of the richest sources of disease-fighting antioxidants. Try to sneak it on to your child's plate whenever possible"

date baby first tried ....

baby's reaction ....

what I thought ....

my variations ....

check
reaction

tomato, sweet potato, and cheese sauce with pasta shells

This delicious sauce is fairly thick and enriched with vegetables. It is also very versatile. You can mix it with pasta, as here, or blend it together with vegetables, fish, or chicken.

- PREPARATION: 10 MINUTES
- COOKING: 30 MINUTES
- MAKES 8 PORTIONS OF SAUCE
- PROVIDES PROTEIN, CALCIUM, BETA-CAROTENE, VITS B_6, C, D, & E, PREBIOTICS
- SAUCE SUITABLE FOR FREEZING

1 tbsp olive oil

1 onion, chopped

1 clove garlic, crushed

2 cups peeled and chopped sweet potatoes

2 medium carrots, peeled and sliced

1 (14oz/400g) can crushed tomatoes

Scant 1 cup boiling vegetable stock or water

½ cup shredded Cheddar cheese

To serve

Mini pasta shells (about 2 heaping tbsp for each portion of sauce)

Heat the oil in a saucepan and sauté the onion until soft, about 4 minutes. Add the garlic and sauté for 1 minute longer. Stir in the sweet potatoes and carrots, then pour in the tomatoes and boiling vegetable stock or water. Bring to a boil, stirring. Cover the pan and simmer until the vegetables are tender, about 30 minutes.

Let cool slightly, then blend the sauce to a purée and stir in the cheese until melted.

Cook the pasta according to the directions on the package. Drain the pasta and mix with the sauce.

" A good way to encourage your baby to chew is to stir mini pasta shapes into his favorite purées. Chewing also helps develop the muscles for speech "

date baby first tried ....

baby's reaction ....

what I thought ....

my variations ....

check
reaction

date baby first tried ....

baby's reaction ....

what I thought ....

my variations ....

check
reaction

perfectly poached chicken

I usually have cooked chicken in my refrigerator, because it is a handy standby for snacks and meals (see below). Poaching is a nice way of cooking chicken breasts, because it helps keep the meat moist.

- PREPARATION: 2 MINUTES
- COOKING: 20–25 MINUTES
- MAKES 4 PORTIONS
- PROVIDES PROTEIN, IRON, ZINC, SELENIUM

1 skinless, boneless chicken breast half (about 5oz/150g)

2½–3 cups chicken stock

Put the chicken breast in a saucepan and add enough stock to cover. Set the pan over medium heat and bring to a boil, then reduce the heat to a very low simmer and poach the chicken for 15 minutes. Turn the breast over and simmer until the chicken is thoroughly cooked, 5–10 minutes longer. To check, make a small cut in the side of the chicken breast and peek in to make sure the meat has turned white all the way through.

Transfer the chicken to a plate (reserve the stock to use in soups and sauces) and cool for 5 minutes, then shred the chicken into small pieces using two forks, going along the grain of the chicken. Cool completely and refrigerate as quickly as possible.

chicken with easy white sauce

- PREPARATION: 5 MINUTES
- COOKING: 10 MINUTES
- MAKES 2 PORTIONS
- PROVIDES PROTEIN, IRON, SELENIUM, CALCIUM, ZINC, FOLATE, VITS A, B_6, & D

½ cup shredded chicken with ⅔ cup of its stock (see above)

1 tbsp butter

1 small shallot, diced

1 tbsp all-purpose flour

3 tbsp heavy cream

2 tbsp frozen green peas

Melt the butter in a pan, add the shallot, and sauté until softened, about 5 minutes. Stir in the flour and cook for 1 minute longer. Remove from the heat. Stir in the stock a little at a time to make a smooth sauce. Return to the heat and slowly bring to a simmer, stirring until thickened. Add the cream, peas, and shredded chicken. Simmer for 2 minutes until everything is hot. Let cool to warm before serving. (Reheat leftovers in the microwave for about 2 minutes, stirring halfway through, until piping hot, then cool.)

cheesy scrambled eggs

Well-cooked scrambled eggs are fine for your baby from around six months—egg allergies are less common than most people think. It's a pity not to give children eggs since they are quick and easy to prepare and very nutritious. If you prefer, leave out the scallion, and try using other types of cheese. Double the quantities for hungry children.

- PREPARATION: 5 MINUTES
- COOKING: 3–4 MINUTES
- MAKES 1 PORTION
- PROVIDES PROTEIN, CALCIUM, VITS C, D, & E

1 egg

1½ tsp milk

2 tsp butter

1 small scallion, sliced

1 small tomato, peeled, seeded, and chopped

2–3 tbsp shredded Cheddar cheese

Beat the egg with the milk. Melt the butter in a medium saucepan and, when foaming, add the scallion and cook for 30 seconds. Add the eggs and chopped tomato and cook gently, stirring, until scrambled. Remove from the heat and sprinkle with the cheese, stirring until it is slightly melted.

creamy zucchini rice

I tend to make this as a quick and easy side dish for pan-grilled or broiled chicken. You could double the quantities and add 2 tsp freshly grated Parmesan cheese if you want to make it a meal in itself.

- PREPARATION: 5 MINUTES
- COOKING: 6–8 MINUTES
- MAKES 1 PORTION
- PROVIDES CALCIUM, FOLATE, VITS A, B_2, & C

¼ medium zucchini

2 tsp butter

3 tbsp cooked rice

2 tbsp milk

Grate the zucchini on the fine side of a box grater. Melt the butter in a saucepan, add the zucchini, and cook gently until the zucchini is soft, about 5–6 minutes. Stir in the rice and milk. Bring up to a simmer and cook until the rice is hot and the milk is almost completely absorbed, 1–2 minutes. Cool slightly before serving.

date baby first tried

baby's reaction

what I thought

my variations

check reaction

date baby first tried

baby's reaction

what I thought

my variations

check reaction

finger-size salmon fishcakes

These fishcakes are breaded so they aren't too squishy to survive being picked up, but for older children (who eat with forks), you could make tablespoon-sized cakes and just dust them in flour before frying. The ketchup in this recipe gives a subtle tang—add more if you like.

- PREPARATION: 25 MINUTES, PLUS OPTIONAL OVERNIGHT CHILLING
- COOKING: ABOUT 4 MINUTES
- MAKES 24–26 (4–6 PORTIONS)
- PROVIDES PROTEIN, OMEGA-3s, IRON, CALCIUM, VITS C, D, & E, POTASSIUM
- SUITABLE FOR FREEZING

I medium potato (about 9oz/250g)

1 recipe Perfectly poached salmon (page 100), or 5oz (150g) store-bought poached salmon, skin removed

1 large or 2 small scallions, finely chopped

1 tbsp mayonnaise

3–4 tsp ketchup (to taste)

2 tbsp all-purpose flour

1 egg, beaten

4 tbsp dry bread crumbs

3 tbsp freshly grated Parmesan cheese

5–6 tbsp sunflower oil, for frying

Microwave the potato until soft, 7–9 minutes (depending on wattage). Let stand for 10 minutes or until cool enough to handle, then peel off the skin with a sharp knife.

Put the potato in a bowl and mash well. Flake the salmon and stir into the potato along with the scallions, mayonnaise, and ketchup. Mix well—you don't want any large pieces of salmon to remain. Roll teaspoonfuls of the mixture into small balls.

Put the flour on a plate; put the egg in a bowl; mix the bread crumbs and Parmesan together on another plate. Dust the balls with flour, then dip in egg and coat in bread crumbs. For best results, cover and chill overnight.

Heat the oil in a frying pan and cook the fishcakes, turning occasionally, until golden brown on all sides, about 4 minutes. Drain on paper towels and let cool to warm before serving.

Note: To freeze, individually freeze, then store in a freezer bag; cook from frozen, adding 1 minute to the cooking time.

date baby first tried ....

baby's reaction ....

what I thought ....

my variations ....

check reaction

date baby first tried ....

baby's reaction ....
....
....

what I thought ....
....
....

my variations ....
....
....
....
....

check reaction

perfectly poached salmon

Try to give your baby omega-3-rich salmon or other oily fish twice a week. Salmon breaks into nice large flakes that are easy to eat.

- PREPARATION: 5 MINUTES
- COOKING: 10 MINUTES
- MAKES 2–3 PORTIONS
- PROVIDES PROTEIN, OMEGA-3s, IRON, SELENIUM, VITS A & E

2 cups vegetable or fish stock

1 piece of salmon fillet with skin, about ¾in (2cm) thick and weighing 5oz (150g)

Put the stock in a medium-sized saucepan and bring up to a simmer. Add the salmon, flesh side down, and cook at a very gentle simmer for 7 minutes. Turn the salmon over and cook until the fish is opaque all the way through and breaks into large flakes when pressed with a fork, about 2–3 minutes longer. (Thicker pieces of salmon may take a few more minutes.)

Transfer the salmon to a plate and let cool slightly before peeling off the skin and scraping away any dark meat (this has a strong flavor that may be a bit much for babies). Break into large flakes to serve.

carrot and orange salad

Coarsely grated carrot is a useful early finger food, because it has a familiar taste and is easy to swallow. You can add 1 tbsp raisins and a few sunflower seeds to make this a tasty salad for older children.

date baby first tried ....

baby's reaction ....
....
....

what I thought ....
....
....

my variations ....
....
....
....
....

check reaction

- PREPARATION: 5 MINUTES, PLUS AT LEAST 1 HOUR CHILLING
- COOKING: NONE
- MAKES 2–3 PORTIONS
- PROVIDES BETA-CAROTENE, VIT C

1 medium carrot, peeled and coarsely grated

2 tsp orange juice

1 tsp olive oil

Salt and pepper

Mix the carrot, juice, and oil together and season with a little pepper (you can add salt for children over 12 months). Cover and chill for at least 1 hour, or overnight, before serving.

poached chicken balls

Traditionally cooked meatballs can be too chewy for first finger foods, but poaching makes them tender and perfect for little ones. The meatballs can be served alone, or with tomato sauce for older children.

- PREPARATION: 25 MINUTES
- COOKING: 4–5 MINUTES
- MAKES ABOUT 20 (4–7 PORTIONS)
- PROVIDES PROTEIN, IRON, ZINC, CALCIUM, SELENIUM, FOLATE, VITS C & D
- SUITABLE FOR FREEZING

1 shallot, diced

1 tsp olive oil

1 cup ground chicken

⅓ cup fresh bread crumbs

¼ sweet apple, peeled and coarsely grated

3 tbsp freshly grated Parmesan cheese

¼ tsp fresh thyme leaves

Pepper

3 cups chicken stock

Sauté the shallot in the oil until softened, about 5–6 minutes. Transfer to a food processor and let cool for 5 minutes. Add the chicken, bread crumbs, apple, Parmesan, and thyme, and season with a little pepper. Process until well-combined. Roll teaspoonfuls of the mixture into small balls.

Put the stock in a saucepan and bring to a boil. Add the chicken balls and poach gently until cooked through, 4–5 minutes. Remove with a slotted spoon and let cool to warm (cut the balls in half for smaller babies).

Note: To reheat a single portion, put the chicken balls in a small bowl and add 1 tsp water. Cover and microwave on high until piping hot, 30–40 seconds. Do not overcook as they will turn rubbery. Cool to warm.

date baby first tried ....

baby's reaction ....

what I thought ....

my variations ....

check reaction

mini oatmeal-raisin cookies

There is something very comforting about the smell of freshly baked cookies wafting through the house. Oats are one of the most nutritious grains, and they help to stabilize blood sugar, giving long-lasting energy. These oatmeal cookies are very quick and easy to prepare, and are fun to make with older children.

- PREPARATION: 15 MINUTES
- COOKING: 10–12 MINUTES
- MAKES ABOUT 18 COOKIES
- PROVIDES IRON, VITS B_1, B_2, B_3, PREBIOTICS
- SUITABLE FOR FREEZING

6 tbsp soft butter

⅓ cup packed light brown sugar

2 tsp light corn syrup or golden syrup

1 tsp pure vanilla extract

⅓ cup all-purpose flour

¼ tsp baking soda

Pinch of salt (not for babies under one year)

1 cup rolled oats

⅓ cup dark raisins, cut in half

Preheat the oven to 350°F (180°C).

Beat the butter, sugar, and corn syrup or golden syrup together with a fork until pale and fluffy, then beat in the vanilla. Fold in the flour, baking soda, salt, and oats, followed by the halved raisins. Form into about 18 small balls and arrange on baking sheets lined with parchment paper.

Bake for 10–12 minutes, rotating the baking sheets halfway through the time. Let cool on the sheets for a few minutes before transferring to a wire rack. The cookies will crisp up as they cool.

meal planner: fingers and spoons

This meal planner provides suggestions for your baby's meals, many of which are drawn from this book. Either use the planner pages to map out your baby's meals for the next weeks or to keep a record of your baby's diet week-by-week.

breakfast	lunch	dinner	extras
My first muesli (p88) fruit	Chicken with easy white sauce (p96) fruit	Tomato, sweet potato, and cheese sauce with pasta shells (pp94–95)	Finger food sandwiches (pp90–92) fruit
scrambled egg and toast fruit	Finger-size salmon fishcakes (pp98–99) with peas yogurt	My favorite chicken purée (p72)	rice cakes fruit
French toast fingers (p89) Apple and pear purée (p58)	Broccoli and cheese baby bites (p93) fruit	My first beef casserole (p71) steamed broccoli and carrot	Mini oatmeal-raisin cookies (pp102–103) fruit
Oatmeal with apple, pear, and apricot (p70) yogurt	Poached chicken balls (p101) Banana smoothie popsicle (p136)	Fillet of fish with cheesy vegetable sauce (pp74–75)	Finger food sandwiches (pp90–92) fruit
cereal Apple and pear purée (p58)	Cheesy scrambled eggs (p97) and toast fingers yogurt	Chicken with easy white sauce (p96) and Creamy zucchini rice (p97) fruit	dried apricots rice cakes
grilled cheese on toast mango or peach	Tomato, sweet potato, and cheese pasta (pp94–95) Strawberry milkshake popsicle (p136)	My favorite chicken purée (p72) with Baked sweet potato purée (p57) fruit	toast fingers with peanut butter vegetable sticks
French toast fingers (p89) yogurt	grilled lamb chops, cut into strips with steamed carrot and cauliflower fruit	Tasty vegetable trio (p68) Banana smoothie popsicle (p136) fruit	Finger food sandwiches (pp90–92) fruit

● healthy breakfasts

Oatmeal provides a great base for introducing new tastes to your baby. Add your baby's favorite fruit purée or mashed fruit for a nutritious breakfast.

WEEK 1	breakfast	lunch	dinner	extras
day 1				
day 2				
day 3				
day 4				
day 5				
day 6				
day 7				

meal planner: weeks 2 and 3

Use these planners to record the meals you give your baby over the following weeks. If you want to record your baby's meals for longer than three weeks, simply photocopy this page. Give your baby pieces of fruit or yogurt as snacks or desserts.

WEEK 2	breakfast	lunch	dinner	extras
day 1				
day 2				
day 3				
day 4				
day 5				
day 6				
day 7				

● lumpier food

Soft pasta shells are great first foods when you're introducing texture and lumpiness to your baby's food. Cold, cooked pasta shapes are good energy-boosting snacks too.

WEEK 3	breakfast	lunch	dinner	extras
day 1				
day 2				
day 3				
day 4				
day 5				
day 6				
day 7				

other favorites

Use this page to write down your other favorite recipes, ideas for snacks and finger foods, good recipes for introducing lumpier foods to your baby, or recipe recommendations from your friends and family. Enjoy experimenting!

chapter 4

toddlers: 12–18 months

"Running around after an energetic toddler can be hard work, so here are some simple but delicious meals and healthy snacks that are quick and easy to prepare."

energy boosters

Toddlers are on the go all the time, whether they're crawling or taking their first uneasy steps, so it's important to keep their energy levels up and provide them with healthy meals and energy-boosting snacks.

Your child's increased independence means that she may become reluctant to sit at the table, so you will need to adapt to her changing needs. This is also a time when your toddler will have much more interaction with other children—at day care or playgroups, for example—and is likely to pick up germs. Healthy, nutrient-packed foods can make all the difference in keeping illnesses at bay and boosting your little one's immunity.

● eating as a family

At 12 months, your child can eat most foods and should be enjoying a full and varied diet. You'll find it will become much easier to include her in family meals. It is important to try to eat together whenever possible since children are more likely to eat if they see you eating too. It's also a good opportunity for your child to try new foods. Many of the recipes in this section are suitable for the whole family as well, such as Chicken parmesan (pages 124–125), Hidden vegetable bolognaise (pages 126–127), Orchard crisp (page 130), and First fruit fool (pages 132–133).

Remember your child still needs to avoid whole nuts, unpasteurized cheese, very salty or spicy foods, and highly refined sugary foods.

● energy-boosting foods

Meals and snacks that give your active toddler a steady stream of energy are vital. Carbohydrates that release sugars slowly into the bloodstream are best. The best sources are rice, potatoes,

a vegetarian diet

✳ **A balanced vegetarian diet** can be very healthy, but it is important to provide the nutrients that meat provides, particularly iron.

✳ **Non-meat sources of iron** include all legumes, fortified whole-grain cereals, and leafy green vegetables, but the iron in these foods is not so readily absorbed as that in red meat.

✳ **Combine these foods** with vitamin C-rich foods or drinks to help absorb the iron, like orange juice alongside breakfast cereal.

✳ **A good vegetarian diet for a child** should include cheese and eggs. Adult vegetarian diets containing bulky foods like whole grains, lentils, and brown rice, are unsuitable for children under the age of two since their tummies will be full before they get all the nutrients they need.

pasta, and whole-grain cereals. They provide long-lasting energy and avoid sudden highs and lows in blood sugar, which can cause mood swings and poor concentration.

● healthy snacks

Your toddler's tummy is little, so don't overload her plate at mealtimes and offer "top-off" snacks when she is hungry again.

Remember that snacks must be nutritious, and not simply quick ways to fill your child's tummy. Dried and fresh fruit, bread sticks, cheese, lean meats, boiled eggs, raw vegetables, yogurt, seeds, toast with peanut butter, hummus, rice cakes, and mini muffins (try the bomb muffins on pages 116–117) are all healthy options and will keep your baby's energy levels up between meals. It's a good idea to have a supply of easy-to-prepare, nutritious snacks on hand, so you aren't tempted to resort to cookies and chocolate.

High-sugar snacks, like cookies, cakes, sugary cereals, and soft drinks, cause a rapid rise in blood sugar. They are perfectly acceptable in small amounts, after or as part of a balanced meal, but when given alone, the body overcompensates for the rapid rise in blood sugar and produces large amounts of insulin, which then causes a dip in blood sugar levels.

● drinks

While it's best to give your child water, a little diluted orange juice at mealtimes will help with iron absorption (especially if she is vegetarian—see box, page 111, for more on this). Always dilute fruit juice (at least three parts water to one part juice), and give juice only at mealtimes.

Children are at greater risk of tooth decay than adults because their newly formed teeth are more vulnerable to acid, so give juice to your child only in a cup and try to do away with bottles by the time

food for the brain

My child is dyspraxic and I've been told that including oily fish in his diet can help. How can I encourage him to eat fish?

It's true that oil-rich fish such as salmon is good for the brain, due to the high level of omega-3 fatty acids. There is overwhelming evidence that increasing the intake of essential fatty acids from oily fish can result in improved concentration, learning, and behavior, and it has been shown to improve the lives of kids with dyslexia, ADHD, and dyspraxia. It's important not to overcook the fish, since overcooking will make it dry, tasteless, and unappetizing (it needs just a few minutes in a pan or microwave). Be sure to remove all bones. Small portions are attractive to kids—try making mini fish pies (page 120) and salmon fishcakes (page 99).

ask annabel

By 12 months
try to do away
with using bottles
and move your baby
to a cup

Broccoli is a true
superfood. It's a good
source of vitamin C
and is packed with
nutrients that help
prevent illness

Fresh fruit
popsicles are a great
way to give more fluids
to your baby when she
is feeling sick

your baby is one; perhaps reserve a bottle of milk for bedtime only. Sweet drinks at bedtime, once the teeth are brushed, are not a good idea since there is not enough saliva in the mouth to wash away harmful acid.

● feeding a sick child

Fluid intake is the main priority over food, so make sure you offer your child drinks at frequent intervals. A good way to give more fluids is to make fresh fruit popsicles for your child to suck on (see recipe on pages 135–137).

If your child has been feverish, try to bring her temperature down before a mealtime. She is extremely unlikely to eat much if she has a high temperature, and is more likely to vomit. If your child refuses the food or becomes distressed, remove the food immediately, trying not to let your stress or disappointment show. Replace the time you would have been feeding your child with a good cuddle or perhaps a massage.

" Your toddler's tummy is little, so don't overload her plate at mealtimes and offer "top-off" snacks when she is hungry again "

When children are sick, they often lose their appetite, which can be worrisome for parents. Parents seem to have a natural instinct to try to feed their children no matter what, but the fact of the matter is that for a few days, children can survive perfectly well on a minuscule amount of food. Their growth rate may slow down or they may even lose a little weight during an illness, but children who are otherwise healthy should make up for this when they feel better.

As your child's appetite returns, offer simple meals and healthy snacks at usual times. Be sure to include energy-boosting, slow-releasing carbohydrates in meals, such as whole-grain cereals, pasta, potatoes, and fruits and vegetables, since you may find that your child is still exhausted days after her other symptoms have disappeared. See "foods to fight illness" (on the following page). Keep things simple, though—after all, this is not the ideal time for you to spend hours in the supermarket or kitchen, experimenting with a new recipe.

If your toddler has been prescribed antibiotics, it's a good idea to give her some live yogurt. Antibiotics kill off the bad and good bacteria in the intestine, but giving your child live yogurt will help to replace the good bacteria.

foods to fight illness

* **Garlic** contains allicin, which is a natural antibiotic, antiviral, and antifungal agent.
* **Vitamin C-rich foods** boost the body's levels of vitamin C, which are depleted during illness, and are thought to reduce cold symptoms. Vitamin C is also needed for the healing of wounds. Good sources include kiwi fruit, citrus fruits, sweet peppers, black currants, dark green leafy vegetables, and strawberries.
* **Apples** are very easy to digest. The BRAT diet (bananas, rice, apples, and toast) is often suggested by doctors for the relief of diarrhea. Pectin, the soluble fiber contained in apples, also helps to relieve constipation. Make sure the apples are peeled.
* **Bananas** are packed full of slow-release sugars for sustained energy. They are also great for diarrhea because they help to bulk the stool. However, they do seem to cause constipation in some susceptible babies.

nutrients to prevent illness

* **Vitamin A**, found in liver, oily fish, milk, cheese, butter, and egg yolks can help prevent infection of the nose, throat, and lungs.
* **Beta-carotene** boosts the immune system against colds and flu. Orange and yellow fruits and vegetables contain high levels. These include carrots, butternut squash, sweet potatoes, rutabagas, cantaloupe, and apricots.
* **Essential fatty acids** such as salmon and other oily fish support brain function and the immune system. Try to give your child oily fish twice a week.
* **Iron**, found in red meats, liver, dried fruits, and iron-enriched cereals, is needed to prevent iron deficiency anemia. This, sadly, is a common condition that is usually preventable, and it makes children more susceptible to frequent infections.

tummy troubles

If your baby hasn't had a bowel movement for more than three days, or her poop is so hard that it causes discomfort, you need to make sure that she drinks plenty of juice, especially prune juice, and water, and include lots of fruit and vegetables in her diet. Give her high-fiber cereals, and avoid excess rice, bananas, and binding foods like macaroni and cheese.

goujons of fish

I like to serve these deliciously crisp goujons with a little ketchup or tartar sauce for dipping.

- PREPARATION: 15–20 MINUTES
- COOKING: 2–3 MINUTES
- MAKES ABOUT 16 (3–4 PORTIONS)
- PROVIDES PROTEIN, IRON, CALCIUM, SELENIUM, VITS B$_6$ & C
- SUITABLE FOR FREEZING

6oz (175g) skinless sole fillets (or similar white fish fillets)

2 tbsp all-purpose flour

About ½ cup Japanese panko (or ordinary dry bread crumbs)

¼ cup freshly grated Parmesan cheese

Finely grated zest of ¼ lemon

⅛ tsp paprika (or to taste)

Salt and pepper

1 egg, beaten with a pinch of salt

4–5 tbsp sunflower oil, for cooking

Pat the fish dry with paper towels and cut into pieces the size of a little finger. Spread the flour out on a large plate. Mix the crumbs, Parmesan, and lemon zest on another large plate and season with the paprika and some salt and pepper. Crack the egg into a small bowl and whisk well.

Toss the fish pieces in the flour and shake off any excess, then dip in the egg and, finally, roll in the crumb mixture.

Heat the oil in a large frying pan or wok over medium heat and fry the goujons until they are golden and the fish is cooked through, 1–1½ minutes on each side. Drain on paper towels and let cool to warm before serving.

Note: To freeze, individually freeze, then transfer to bags; fry from frozen, allowing 30 seconds extra cooking time.

date baby first tried ....

baby's reaction ....
....
....
....

what I thought ....
....
....

my variations ....
....
....
....
....
....

check reaction

date baby first tried ....

baby's reaction ....

....

....

....

what I thought ....

....

....

....

my variations ....

....

....

....

....

....

check reaction

> Just one serving of blueberries provides as many disease-fighting antioxidants as five servings of carrots, apples, squash, or broccoli

bomb muffins (banana, oat, maple, and blueberry)

If your baby doesn't care too much for texture, put the ingredients for the muffin batter in a food processor and process until smooth, then add the blueberries and pulse three or four times to chop.

- PREPARATION: 15–20 MINUTES
- COOKING: 12–14 MINUTES
- MAKES 18 MINI OR 9 REGULAR MUFFINS
- PROVIDES POTASSIUM, VITS A, B_3, & C, PREBIOTICS
- SUITABLE FOR FREEZING

6 tbsp rolled oats

⅔ cup whole-wheat flour

½ tsp baking soda

½ tsp baking powder

½ tsp ground cinnamon

½ tsp ground ginger

¼ tsp salt

1 very ripe banana, mashed

1 egg

2 tbsp butter, melted

¼ cup maple syrup

3 tbsp light brown sugar

¾ tsp pure vanilla extract

⅓ cup blueberries

1 tbsp Turbinado (raw) or maple sugar

Preheat the oven to 350°F (180°C). Line 18 cups of two mini muffin pans with paper muffin cups.

Mix together the oats, flour, baking soda, baking powder, cinnamon, ginger, and salt in a large bowl. In a separate bowl, mix together the banana, egg, butter, syrup, brown sugar, and vanilla. Mix the wet ingredients into the dry until just combined, then add in the blueberries.

Spoon into the muffin cups, filling them three-quarters full. Sprinkle a little Turbinado (raw) sugar on each muffin. Bake until risen and firm to the touch, 12–14 minutes. Cool on a wire rack.

Note: If frozen, remove the muffins as needed and thaw for 30 minutes at room temperature.

Variation: If you don't have mini muffin pans, you can make nine regular size muffins, which will take 15–17 minutes to bake. Cut the muffins into cubes or small pieces for toddlers.

baked pita chips

These are handy for snacks—and healthier than potato chips. Store them in an airtight container. The cinnamon-sugar pita chips taste even better dipped into yogurt.

parmesan and herb pita chips

● PREPARATION: 10 MINUTES
● COOKING: 8–10 MINUTES
● MAKES 16 CHIPS
● PROVIDES CALCIUM, VITS B_1, & B_3

2 small (or 1 large) whole-wheat or plain pita breads

1 tbsp olive oil, plus extra for greasing

3 tbsp freshly grated Parmesan cheese

½ tsp chopped fresh thyme (optional)

Preheat the oven to 350°F (180°C).

Cut the pitas into quarters (cut large pitas into eighths) and peel the pieces apart to get 16 triangles. Brush both sides of each triangle with olive oil (you may not need all of the oil) and set, smooth side down, on a lightly greased baking sheet. Sprinkle with the Parmesan and thyme (if using). Bake for 8–10 minutes, watching carefully after the first 6 minutes to be sure the chips do not brown too much. Cool on a wire rack.

cinnamon-sugar pita chips

● PREPARATION: 10–15 MINUTES
● COOKING: ABOUT 20 MINUTES
● MAKES 16 CHIPS
● PROVIDES VITS A, B_1 & B_3 (NIACIN)

2 small (or 1 large) whole-wheat or plain pita breads

2 tbsp butter

2 tsp light brown sugar

½ tsp ground cinnamon

Preheat the oven to 275°F (140°C).

Cut the pitas into quarters (cut large pitas into eighths) and peel the pieces apart to get 16 triangles. Put the butter, sugar, and cinnamon in a small saucepan and stir over low heat until melted. Brush both sides of the pita triangles generously with the butter mixture (you may not need all of it) and set on a baking sheet lined with parchment paper. Bake for 10 minutes, then turn the chips over and bake for 9–10 minutes longer. Cool on a wire rack—they will crisp up as they cool.

tuna tortilla melt

Tuna is a true superfood standby, rich in protein and vitamins (I prefer tuna packed in oil rather than brine). The good thing about a tortilla sandwich is that it is nice and thin—and easily grasped by little ones.

- PREPARATION: 5 MINUTES
- COOKING: 2–4 MINUTES
- MAKES 1 LARGE PORTION
- PROVIDES PROTEIN, CALCIUM, IRON, SELENIUM, VITS A, C, & D

⅓–½ cup canned tuna, drained

1 tbsp sour cream

2 tsp ketchup

2–3 drops of lemon juice

1 scallion, finely chopped

¼ cup shredded Cheddar cheese

1 small flour tortilla wrap

If using the broiler to cook the sandwich, preheat it. Mix the tuna, sour cream, ketchup, lemon juice, and scallion together. Stir in the cheese. Spread the mixture on half of the tortilla, then fold the other half overtop. Toast under the broiler or in a dry frying pan until crisp and browned, 1–2 minutes on each side. Cool to warm before cutting and serving.

toasted peanut butter and banana sandwich

Protein-rich peanut butter and banana make a very dynamic duo! I like to roll out the bread so that the sandwich is a little thinner and easier to eat. Make half a sandwich if your child has a small appetite.

- PREPARATION: 5 MINUTES
- COOKING: ABOUT 4 MINUTES
- MAKES 1 LARGE PORTION
- PROVIDES PROTEIN, MAGNESIUM, POTASSIUM, VITS A, B$_1$, B$_3$, & E

1 rounded tbsp smooth peanut butter

2 slices bread, flattened

½ small banana, mashed

1 tbsp soft butter

Preheat the broiler. Spread the peanut butter over the bread, then spread the banana on top of one slice and put the other slice on top. Spread the butter in a thin layer over the outside of both sides of the sandwich, going right to the edges. Toast under the broiler until crisp and golden, about 2 minutes on each side. Cool to warm, then cut into fingers.

date baby first tried...................................

baby's reaction ....

what I thought ....

my variations ....

check reaction

date baby first tried...................................

baby's reaction ....

what I thought ....

my variations ....

check reaction

date baby first tried ....

baby's reaction ....

....
....
....
....

what I thought ....

....
....
....

my variations ....

....
....
....
....
....
....
....

check
reaction

first fish pie

I like to keep cubes of puréed squash in the freezer as a standby vegetable and they are also useful for adding to sauces. To make the purée from scratch, you need to steam about 1 cup peeled and cubed butternut squash for 8–10 minutes until soft, then mash or purée in a blender or food processor.

- PREPARATION: 30 MINUTES
- COOKING: 20–25 MINUTES
- MAKES 4–6 INDIVIDUAL PIES
- PROVIDES PROTEIN, CALCIUM, SELENIUM, IRON, BETA-CAROTENE, VITS A, C, D, & E
- SUITABLE FOR FREEZING

9oz (250g) skinless cod fillet
(or similar white fish), cubed

Topping

1lb (450g) potatoes, peeled and cubed
(about 3½ cups)

1 tbsp butter

3 tbsp milk

Salt and pepper

Sauce

2 tsp butter

2 tsp all-purpose flour

²/₃ cup milk

¾ cup butternut squash purée
(see above)

½ cup shredded sharp Cheddar
cheese

2 tbsp freshly grated Parmesan
cheese

Divide the cubed fish among four to six small ovenproof dishes or ramekins.

Cook the potatoes in plenty of boiling water until just tender, about 15 minutes. Drain the potatoes, then mash well. Beat in the butter and milk, and season to taste with salt and pepper.

Make the sauce while the potatoes are cooking. Melt the butter in a small saucepan, then stir in the flour and cook for 1 minute. Remove from the heat and gradually stir in the milk until you have a smooth sauce. Return to low heat and cook, stirring constantly, until the sauce comes to a boil and thickens. Stir in the squash purée, then remove from the heat and stir in the cheeses until melted. Cool slightly before spooning over the fish.

Preheat the oven to 400°F (200°C). Spoon the mashed potatoes over the fish and sauce, and use a fork to mark the surface with ridges.

Set the dish(es) on a baking sheet and bake until hot in the center and golden on top, about 20 minutes. If the pies have come straight from the refrigerator, bake them for an extra 5 minutes. The tops can be browned further under the broiler, if you like.

Note: To freeze, wrap the unbaked potato-topped pies well; thaw overnight in the refrigerator before baking.

date baby first tried ....

baby's reaction ....
....
....
....
....

what I thought ....
....
....

my variations ....
....
....
....
....
....
....

check
reaction

cheese and pea orzo

Orzo, which is small rice-shaped pasta, is easy to swallow and good for smaller children (use star-shaped or other small pasta shapes if you cannot find orzo). This dish is quite "sticky" when cooked, so is useful for toddlers who are trying to use a spoon or fork—there's a good chance some will stay on the utensil and reach the mouth!

● PREPARATION: 5 MINUTES
● COOKING: 12–15 MINUTES
● MAKES 1 PORTION
● PROVIDES PROTEIN, POTASSIUM,
   CALCIUM, FOLATE, VITS A, C, & D

2 tbsp orzo

1 tbsp frozen green peas

1 tbsp heavy cream

3 tbsp finely grated Cheddar cheese

1 tsp freshly grated Parmesan cheese

Cook the orzo according to package directions (you can use vegetable stock instead of water for more flavor). Add the peas for the final minute of cooking. Drain well and return the orzo and peas to the saucepan over low heat.

Stir in the heavy cream and simmer for a couple of minutes until almost fully absorbed. Remove from the heat and stir in the Cheddar cheese until melted. Cool slightly to warm before serving with the Parmesan.

quick chicken risotto

If you are in a real hurry, then you can omit the shallot and broccoli and just add 1 tbsp green peas with the chicken.

- PREPARATION: 5–10 MINUTES
- COOKING: 8–10 MINUTES
- MAKES 1 PORTION
- PROVIDES PROTEIN, IRON, ZINC, FOLATE, SELENIUM, VITS A, B$_3$, B$_{12}$, C, & D

1 tsp butter

1 tsp finely diced shallot

½ cup small broccoli florets

⅓ cup cooked rice

¼ cup chicken stock

3–4 tbsp shredded cooked chicken (see page 96)

1 tbsp freshly grated Parmesan cheese

Melt the butter in a small saucepan and sauté the shallot until softened, 5–6 minutes. Meanwhile, steam the broccoli until just tender, 3–4 minutes.

Add the rice, stock, chicken, and cooked broccoli to the saucepan and simmer until most of the stock has been absorbed, 2–3 minutes. Remove from the heat and stir in the Parmesan.

pasta with simple squash and cheese sauce

If you keep cubes of butternut squash purée in the freezer, you can thaw one and whip up this sauce in no time (see page 56 for how to make the purée from scratch). You could add a splash of heavy cream, if you have any in the refrigerator.

- PREPARATION: 5 MINUTES
- COOKING: 10–12 MINUTES
- MAKES 1 PORTION
- PROVIDES PROTEIN, CALCIUM, BETA-CAROTENE, VITS A, D, & E

3 tbsp small pasta shapes or macaroni noodles

2 tbsp butternut squash purée (see above)

2 tbsp milk

¼ cup grated Gruyère or Cheddar cheese

Salt and pepper

Cook the pasta according to package directions. Drain and return to the pan over low heat. Add the squash purée and milk, and stir until hot. Remove from the heat and stir in the cheese until melted. Season to taste.

date baby first tried ....

baby's reaction ....

what I thought ....

my variations ....

check reaction

date baby first tried ....

baby's reaction ....

what I thought ....

my variations ....

check reaction

chicken parmesan

I would defy even the fussiest child to reject this dish, since it checks all of the right boxes for baby tastebuds—breaded chicken, tomato sauce, and melted cheese. It is a great dish to grow up with—just cut the cooked chicken into pieces suitable for your child's age and teeth.

- PREPARATION: 10–15 MINUTES
- COOKING: 30 MINUTES
- MAKES 4 PORTIONS
- PROVIDES PROTEIN, IRON, SELENIUM, ZINC, CALCIUM, VITS C, D, & E, PREBIOTICS
- SUITABLE FOR FREEZING

1 large shallot, diced

1 tbsp olive oil

1 small clove garlic, crushed

1 (14oz/400g) can crushed tomatoes

1½ tbsp tomato paste

1 tsp sugar

Salt and pepper

2 skinless, boneless chicken breast halves (about 5oz/150g each)

1 egg, beaten

2 tbsp all-purpose flour

½ cup dry bread crumbs

3–4 tbsp sunflower oil, for frying

½ cup shredded mozzarella cheese

2 tbsp freshly grated Parmesan cheese

Put the shallot and olive oil in a wok or large pan and sauté until softened, 4–5 minutes. Add the garlic and cook for 1 minute, then stir in the tomatoes, tomato paste, and sugar. Simmer until thick, about 20–25 minutes. Season to taste. Remove from the heat and blend to a purée. Keep warm.

While the sauce is simmering, cut the chicken breasts in half horizontally and lay each half out flat. Cover with plastic wrap and beat out until about ¼in (5mm) thick. Put the egg in a bowl; spread the flour on a large plate; spread the bread crumbs on a second large plate and season them. Dust the flattened chicken breast halves with flour, then dip in the egg, and, finally, coat with the bread crumbs.

Heat the sunflower oil in a large nonstick frying pan and cook the chicken breasts over medium heat until the chicken is just cooked and the coating is golden brown, about 3 minutes on each side. Drain briefly on paper towels and transfer to a baking dish. Preheat the broiler.

Spread about 3 tbsp of tomato sauce over each chicken breast and scatter the mozzarella and Parmesan on top. Broil, 2–3in (5–7cm) from the heat, until the cheese is bubbling, 3–4 minutes. Cool slightly before serving.

Note: Freeze the sauce and coated chicken separately. Cook the chicken from frozen, adding an extra 1–2 minutes per side to the cooking time; reheat the sauce and complete the recipe.

hidden vegetable bolognaise

If your child won't eat vegetables, then bolognaise is a good way to hide them. The apple is an unusual ingredient, but adds a sweetness that children enjoy. Serve with spaghetti or other pasta, or with rice.

- PREPARATION: 15 MINUTES
- COOKING: 1 HOUR
- MAKES 8 PORTIONS
- PROVIDES PROTEIN, IRON, SELENIUM, ZINC, BETA-CAROTENE, FOLATE, VITS B$_2$, B$_3$, & C, PREBIOTICS
- SUITABLE FOR FREEZING

1 tbsp olive oil

1 small onion, finely chopped

1 small leek, thinly sliced

½ stalk celery, diced

¼ small red bell pepper, diced

1 small carrot, peeled and grated

½ sweet apple, peeled and grated

1 clove garlic, crushed

1 (14oz/400g) can crushed tomatoes

1lb (450g) ground beef

¼ cup tomato paste

2 tbsp ketchup

1 cup beef stock

¼ tsp dried oregano

Salt and pepper

Heat the oil in a large frying pan and sauté the vegetables, apple, and garlic until soft, about 10 minutes. Transfer to a blender and add the tomatoes, then blend until smooth.

Wipe out the pan with a paper towel, then add the ground beef and cook over medium-high heat, breaking up the meat with a wooden spoon, until browned and crumbly (you may need to do this in two batches). If your child likes a finer texture, you can transfer the browned beef to a food processor; pulse the machine on and off until the beef is well-chopped.

Add the tomato and vegetable sauce to the beef and stir in the tomato paste, ketchup, stock, and oregano. Bring up to a simmer and cook until the sauce has thickened, 40–45 minutes. Season to taste with salt and pepper.

date baby first tried ....

baby's reaction ....

what I thought ....

my variations ....

check reaction

This sauce is so versatile. Try mixing it with fusilli, top with béchamel sauce, sprinkle with grated cheese, and brown under the grill

date baby first tried ....

baby's reaction ....
....
....
....
....
....

what I thought ....
....
....
....

my variations ....
....
....
....
....
....
....
....

check
reaction

crunchy tofu cubes

Tofu is a good source of protein and its fairly soft texture makes it a good food for babies with few teeth. Vegans can omit the flour and egg part of the coating and just roll the marinated tofu cubes in bread crumbs. However, you will need to cook the crumbed tofu immediately, because the crumbs will become soggy if left standing. Also, the cubes will be a bit softer and less easy to pick up than the traditionally breaded version. Note that this recipe is for toddlers over one year —the salt in soy sauce is unsuitable for younger children.

- PREPARATION: 15–20 MINUTES, PLUS MINIMUM 8 HOURS MARINATING
- COOKING: 6 MINUTES
- MAKES 16 CUBES
- PROVIDES PROTEIN, CALCIUM, VITS D & E

9oz (250g) extra-firm tofu, cut into ¾in (2cm) cubes

½ tsp grated fresh ginger

2 tsp soy sauce

1 tsp mirin

1 tsp clear honey

2 tbsp all-purpose flour

1 egg, lightly beaten

½ cup dry bread crumbs (preferably honey panko)

5 tbsp sunflower oil, for frying

Blot as much excess liquid as possible from the tofu cubes, using paper towels. Mix the ginger, soy sauce, mirin, and honey together in a bowl. Add the tofu and toss to coat, then cover and let marinate in the refrigerator for 8 hours or overnight, turning the cubes once or twice.

Put the flour and egg in separate bowls and spread the bread crumbs on a large plate. Remove the tofu cubes from the marinade, then dust with flour, dip in egg, and roll in bread crumbs.

Put a thin layer of oil in a large nonstick frying pan and heat until shimmering. Drop a couple of bread crumbs into the oil—if they sizzle immediately, the oil is hot enough. Fry the tofu cubes until golden brown all over, about 30–40 seconds on each side. Drain on paper towels and let cool until warm before serving. Alternatively, you can serve these cold as well.

ginger cookie shapes

It is fun to use various novelty cutters, such as stars, circles, and flowers, so that your baby can learn the names of the shapes.

- PREPARATION: 25–30 MINUTES, PLUS 1–2 HOURS CHILLING
- COOKING: ABOUT 9 MINUTES
- MAKES ABOUT 30 COOKIES
- PROVIDES VITS A & E

3 tbsp butter, softened

⅓ cup packed light brown sugar

¼ cup light corn syrup or golden syrup

1 extra large egg yolk

1 cup + 3 tbsp all-purpose flour

2 tsp ground ginger

½ tsp baking soda

¼ tsp salt

Beat the butter and sugar together until pale and fluffy, then beat in the corn syrup or golden syrup and egg yolk until just combined. Sift the flour, ginger, baking soda, and salt over the top, and stir in with a wooden spoon to form a dough. Put the dough on a piece of plastic wrap and pat into a disk about ½in (1.25cm) thick. Wrap up and refrigerate for 1–2 hours until firm.

Preheat the oven to 350°F (180°C). Roll out the dough between two pieces of parchment paper until about ⅛in (3mm) thick. Cut out shapes about 2in (5cm) in diameter, and use a metal spatula to transfer them to baking sheets lined with parchment paper. If the dough becomes too soft, then lift it, still on the parchment, onto a baking sheet and freeze for 5–10 minutes to firm up.

Bake the cookies until they have puffed up and are just turning golden around the edges, about 9 minutes. For crisper cookies, bake for an extra 2 minutes. Let cool on the baking sheet for 5 minutes, then transfer to a wire rack to cool completely. Store in an airtight container.

date baby first tried ....

baby's reaction ....
....
....
....

what I thought ....
....
....

my variations ....
....
....
....
....
....

check reaction

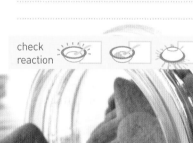

date baby first tried ....

baby's reaction ....

....

....

....

what I thought ....

....

....

my variations ....

....

....

....

....

....

....

check reaction

orchard crisp

These easy individual crisps are very popular. To vary them, you can use smaller apples and pears and throw in a few blackberries for the last 2 minutes when cooking the fruit.

- PREPARATION: 15–20 MINUTES
- COOKING: 20–25 MINUTES
- MAKES 4 PORTIONS
- PROVIDES FOLATE, VITS A & C, POTASSIUM
- SUITABLE FOR FREEZING

2 large sweet apples (e.g., Golden Delicious), peeled, cored, and diced

2 large pears (e.g., Anjou), peeled, cored, and diced

$2/3$ cup all-purpose flour

3 tbsp butter, cut into cubes

$1/4$ cup Turbinado (raw) sugar

$3/4$ tsp ground cinnamon

$1/4$ tsp salt

4 tsp sugar, or to taste

Preheat the oven to 400°F (200°C).

Put the fruit in a small saucepan and cook gently until softened but not mushy, 10–15 minutes.

Meanwhile, put the flour in a bowl and rub in the butter until it looks like crumbs. Stir in the Turbinado sugar, cinnamon, and salt.

Remove the fruit from the heat and stir in the sugar, adding more if the fruit isn't sweet enough. Divide the fruit among four ramekins (about 3¾in/9cm in diameter) and sprinkle the crumb mixture over the top. Bake for 20–25 minutes. Cool to warm before serving, with ice cream, if desired.

Note: To freeze, cool the baked crisps and wrap well; thaw overnight in the refrigerator, then reheat in the microwave for 1–2 minutes.

bananas "foster"

Who can resist bananas in a warm caramel sauce? Remember that hot sugar can take a while to cool down, so please be sure to check the temperature of the sauce before serving to small children.

- PREPARATION: 5 MINUTES
- COOKING: 2 MINUTES
- MAKES 2 PORTIONS
- PROVIDES POTASSIUM, VIT A (PLUS VIT D AND CALCIUM IF SERVED WITH ICE CREAM)

1 large, slightly underripe banana

1 tbsp butter

1 tbsp maple syrup

1 tbsp light brown sugar

Pinch of ground cinnamon (optional)

Peel the banana and cut it in half crosswise, then in half again lengthwise. Put the butter, syrup, sugar, and cinnamon in a small nonstick frying pan. Melt over low heat. Stir well, then increase the heat to medium. When the syrup is boiling, add the banana pieces, cut side down. Cook for 1 minute, then carefully turn the pieces over and cook for 1 minute longer.

Lift the bananas into serving bowls and spoon the sauce over them. Let cool to warm before serving with vanilla ice cream. (The bananas can be kept in the refrigerator for 24 hours; reheat in the microwave for 1 minute.)

coconut rice pudding

You can serve this warm or chilled, but I prefer it chilled. The rice tends to set as it chills, so you may need to add some cream to soften it up.

- PREPARATION: 10 MINUTES
- COOKING: 20 MINUTES
- MAKES 3–4 PORTIONS
- PROVIDES VITS A, D, & E (PLUS ADDITIONAL VITS DEPENDING ON FRUIT PURÉE USED)

1/3 cup jasmine rice

Scant 1 cup (7 fl oz) whole milk

Scant 1 cup (7 fl oz) coconut milk

1–2 tsp sugar (to taste)

2–3 drops of pure vanilla extract

To serve cold

5 tbsp heavy cream

3 tbsp mango or other fruit purée

Put the rice, milk, and coconut milk into a medium saucepan. Bring to a boil, then simmer, stirring occasionally, until the rice is tender, about 20 minutes. Remove from the heat and stir in the sugar and vanilla.

If serving cold, stir 1 tbsp of the cream into the chilled rice to loosen it. Whip the remaining cream and fold in. Swirl mango purée over the top.

date baby first tried ....

baby's reaction ....

....

....

....

....

what I thought ....

....

....

....

my variations ....

....

....

....

....

....

....

check
reaction

first fruit fool

Even fussy babies usually like a combination of sweet fruit mixed with creamy yogurt. Adults love this too, so you may need to make double!

- PREPARATION: 10 MINUTES
- COOKING: NONE
- MAKES 4 PORTIONS
- PROVIDES CALCIUM, FOLATE, VITS B$_1$, C, D, & E

1 cup quartered strawberries

1 cup raspberries

1 tbsp sugar

1 cup heavy cream

½ tsp pure vanilla extract

1 tsp confectioners' (powdered) sugar

¼ cup thick (Greek-style) plain yogurt

2 gingersnap cookies (optional)

Purée the berries with the sugar in a blender or food processor. Taste for sweetness and add a little more sugar, if necessary. Strain the purée to remove the seeds and set aside. Whip the cream with the vanilla and confectioners' sugar until it holds soft peaks. Gently fold in the yogurt, then stir through the purée—it is nice to leave the purée slightly marbled in the cream mixture.

Spoon into small glasses, cover, and refrigerate until needed. (The fools can be kept in the refrigerator for up to 2 days.) If you like ginger, then these are even better with gingersnap cookies crumbled on top just before serving, although smaller babies may prefer it without the cookie crumbs.

date baby first tried ....

baby's reaction ....
....
....
....
....

what I thought ....
....
....

my variations ....
....
....
....
....
....
....
....

check reaction

my favorite frozen yogurt

I love frozen yogurt, and this tastes so good that you don't really need any extra flavorings. However, if you like, you could add a fruit purée such as the summer berry flavor below. For best results, make the frozen yogurt in an ice-cream machine, although you can also make it without. Simply put the mixture in a suitable container in the freezer, and then process in an electric mixer or food processor two or three times during the freezing process to break up the ice crystals.

- PREPARATION: 30 MINUTES (INCLUDING CHURNING), PLUS 3–4 HOURS FREEZING
- COOKING: NONE
- MAKES ABOUT 3 CUPS
- PROVIDES CALCIUM, VITS A, D, & E

2 cups whole-milk plain yogurt
1 cup heavy cream
½ cup sugar

Simply mix all the ingredients together and freeze in an ice-cream machine. Transfer to a suitable container and keep in the freezer. If possible, remove from the freezer about 10 minutes before serving.

Variation: Summer berry frozen yogurt

Gently simmer about 2 cups fresh or frozen berries (e.g., strawberries, raspberries, blueberries, or blackberries) with about 2 tbsp confectioners' (powdered) sugar to taste, then purée in a blender. Press through a strainer to remove the seeds. Mix the fruit purée with the yogurt mixture before freezing in an ice-cream machine. Alternatively, omit the cooking and just purée fresh berries, then strain and beat in about 2 tbsp confectioners' sugar to sweeten. Makes about 3½ cups.

" Try mixing other flavors into the yogurt base. Use a mango purée, mixed with a little sugar, or sieve some canned lychees to make a delicious lychee frozen yogurt "

raspberry ripple popsicles

Sucking on a popsicle will help soothe sore gums when your child is teething. It's also good if your child is feeling sick and not eating well, preventing her from becoming dehydrated. But then who needs an excuse to eat this yummy confection of frozen yogurt rippled with fresh raspberry purée? I have beaten the yogurt mixture to improve the texture, but this is optional.

- PREPARATION: 15–20 MINUTES, PLUS OVERNIGHT FREEZING
- COOKING: NONE
- MAKES ABOUT 2½ CUPS
- PROVIDES CALCIUM, FOLATE, VITS C, D & E

1½ cups raspberries
⅓ cup confectioners' (powdered) sugar
1½ cups vanilla yogurt
¾ cup heavy cream

Purée the raspberries with 2 tbsp of the confectioners' sugar in a blender or food processor. Strain to remove the seeds and set aside.

Mix the yogurt, cream, and remaining confectioners' sugar in a large bowl. Beat with an electric mixer until thick and increased by about half in volume, 1–2 minutes.

Stir 6 tbsp of the yogurt mixture into the raspberry purée. Spoon this raspberry mixture onto the yogurt mixture and roughly ripple through using the blade of a knife (don't overmix, because it will mix a bit more as you pour it). Spoon or pour into popsicle molds and freeze.

strawberry-cranberry popsicles

The strawberry is packed with vitamin C! If your strawberries are very ripe, then you may need slightly less sugar.

- PREPARATION: 8–10 MINUTES, PLUS OVERNIGHT FREEZING
- COOKING: NONE
- MAKES ABOUT 2½ CUPS
- PROVIDES BETA-CAROTENE, FOLATE, VITS B$_1$, B$_2$, B$_3$ (NIACIN), & C

1 lb (450g) strawberries, quartered (about 4 cups)
1¼ cups cranberry juice
½ cup confectioners' (powdered) sugar, sifted

Blend the strawberries, cranberry juice, and sugar together in a blender until smooth. Strain to remove any seeds, then spoon or pour into popsicle molds and freeze.

date baby first tried

baby's reaction

what I thought

my variations

check reaction

date baby first tried

baby's reaction

what I thought

my variations

check reaction

date baby first tried ....

baby's reaction ....

....

....

what I thought ....

....

....

my variations ....

....

....

....

check
reaction

date baby first tried ....

baby's reaction ....

....

....

....

what I thought ....

....

....

my variations ....

....

....

check
reaction

banana smoothie popsicles

This is a good way to use up the overripe bananas that always seem to be hiding in the bottom of the fruit bowl. For a special treat, you can add a little dulce de leche (a South American milk-based syrup) to the mix, or dip the popsicles in a little melted chocolate as you eat them.

- PREPARATION: 5 MINUTES, PLUS OVERNIGHT FREEZING
- COOKING: NONE
- MAKES ABOUT 2 CUPS
- PROVIDES CALCIUM, POTASSIUM, VITS A, C, D, & E

2 large, ripe bananas, peeled

¾ cup vanilla yogurt

Scant 1 cup milk

Blend the bananas and yogurt together in a blender until smooth, then add the milk and blend to combine. Pour into popsicle molds and freeze.

strawberry milkshake popsicles

I like to make this using probiotic strawberry yogurt drinks.

- PREPARATION: 8–10 MINUTES, PLUS OVERNIGHT FREEZING
- COOKING: NONE
- MAKES ABOUT 2½ CUPS
- PROVIDES CALCIUM, VITS A, C, & D

2 cups strawberries, quartered

1½ cups strawberry yogurt

½ cup milk

3 tbsp confectioners' (powdered) sugar, sifted

Use a blender to reduce the strawberries to a purée. Add the remaining ingredients and blend until frothy. Strain to remove the strawberry seeds, then pour into popsicle molds and freeze.

" Babies who are teething are often reluctant to eat. Sucking on an enticing popsicle can be good since it helps to soothe sore gums "

meal planner: energy boosters

This meal planner provides suggestions for your toddler's meals, many of which are drawn from this book. Either use the planner pages to map out your toddler's meals for the next weeks or to keep a record of your child's diet week-by-week.

breakfast	lunch	dinner	extras
oatmeal with honey fruit	First fish pie (pp120–121) fruit	Muffin pizza with hidden vegetable tomato sauce (pp152–152) First fruit fool (pp132–133)	Parmesan and herb pita chips (p118); carrot and cucumber sticks and dip e.g., hummus
scrambled egg on whole-grain toast fruit	Pasta with simple squash and cheese sauce (p123) fruit	Chicken parmesan (pp124–125) Bananas "foster" (p131)	Finger food sandwiches (pp90–92) yogurt
cereal fruit smoothie yogurt or dried fruit	Hidden vegetable bolognaise with pasta (pp126–127); Strawberry-cranberry popsicle (p135)	Goujons of fish (p115) with oven-baked fries and peas Orchard crisp (p130)	Parmesan and herb pita chips (p118); carrot and cucumber sticks and dip e.g., hummus
French toast fingers (p89) mango or peach	Quick chicken risotto (p123) Orchard crisp (p130)	Muffin pizza with hidden vegetable tomato sauce (p152); Coconut rice pudding (p131)	Toasted peanut butter and banana sandwich (p119) yogurt
wheat-based cereal banana	Cheese and pea orzo (p122) First fruit fool (pp132–133)	Cute cottage pie (p169) fruit	Bomb (banana, oats, maple, and blueberry) muffin (pp116–117) fruit
toast fruit yogurt	Tuna tortilla melt (p119) My favorite frozen yogurt (p134) fruit	Hidden vegetable bolognaise with pasta (pp126–127); Raspberry ripple popsicle (p135)	dried fruit e.g., apricots and raisins yogurt
Cheesy scrambled eggs (p97) fruit	Toasted peanut butter and banana sandwich (p119) fruit	My first sweet and sour pork (p164) Strawberry milkshake popsicle (p136)	Ginger cookie shapes (p129) yogurt fruit

● fishy favorites

Goujons of fish (p115) are a great way to tempt your little one into eating fish. They can be cooked from frozen too—perfect for when you're short on time.

WEEK 1	breakfast	lunch	dinner	extras
day 1				
day 2				
day 3				
day 4				
day 5				
day 6				
day 7				

meal planner: weeks 2 and 3

Use these planners to record the meals you give your toddler over the following weeks. If you want to record your child's meals for longer than three weeks, simply photocopy this page. Pieces of fruit or yogurt are good for snacks or desserts.

WEEK 2	breakfast	lunch	dinner	extras
day 1				
day 2				
day 3				
day 4				
day 5				
day 6				
day 7				

● **individual portions**

Your child will love individual child-sized
portions of foods, such as My first fruit fool,
right (see pages 132–133) and First fish pie
(see pages 120–121).

WEEK 3	breakfast	lunch	dinner	extras
day 1				
day 2				
day 3				
day 4				
day 5				
day 6				
day 7				

other favorites

Use this page to write down your other favorite recipes, ideas for healthy and energy-boosting snacks, or recipe recommendations from your friends and family. It will be much easier to include your child in family meals, so enjoy experimenting!

foods my child loves and hates

Children have preferences from a young age. If your child rejects a food, try it again in a few weeks, in a totally different recipe.

Use this page to record your child's likes and dislikes. You'll find it will be amusing to look back on in years to come.

chapter 5

fussy eaters: 18–36 months

"Almost all children go through a stage of fussy eating. This can be very stressful, so here are my top tips on how to cope and some favorite recipes to tempt your child that the whole family can enjoy."

healthy habits

Children of this age have a strong sense of self and can be fiercely independent. They often insist on having their own way, so you may find that your child, who used to eat so well, suddenly becomes very picky.

Don't despair, though, as your child gets a little older, you may find that he becomes more appreciative of food and can be completely absorbed by the food he eats. You'll be surprised how quiet a group of children can be around a table of yummy goodies or a birthday party spread.

● coping with a fussy eater

Whether they reject random recipes with butternut squash, visible onions, "hidden" zucchini, "naked" chicken without breadcrumbs,

or chocolate brownies with nuts, let's face it, fuss is high on the menu for most children. Refusing foods is a normal part of growing up and is one of the first ways children can flex their muscles and assert their independence.

One thing is for sure—if your child refuses to eat, he will soon find that there is not much point making a fuss if you don't react. The problem is that this is stressful for you, and you need to pretend that you actually don't care at all. Remove uneaten food without comment and offer nothing, despite the screams, tears, and tantrums. This will be difficult to handle, but it's not cruel. When it works, you should have a happier, healthier child (and be less frazzled yourself). You will need help and support with this, so the whole family has to be in agreement and stick to the plan (even grandma!). Praise your child when he eats well or tries something new. You may need to ignore some bad eating behavior to refocus attention on good behavior.

● faddy eating

Many children go through phases of refusing to eat certain foods or refusing to eat anything at all. If your child only wants to eat a few favorite foods, try to build on a favorite food and work in others. If your child likes pasta, for example, make noodles with vegetables and chicken or spaghetti with meatballs.

It is very rare for a healthy child to starve himself. Even if your child goes through a few days of virtually eating nothing, he should start eating again very soon. He won't harm himself if he doesn't eat for a short while. The best thing to do is offer a wide range of healthy, tasty meals—don't let your child pick. Also, cut out all unhealthy foods and minimize snacks.

● making vegetables tempting

Vegetables come pretty much on top of the hate list and it may seem impossible to get your child to eat his five-a-day, when he won't even eat one or two. Here are some suggestions:

✳ **Finger foods** are popular with kids. Corn on the cob and sweet potato wedges are good choices.

✳ **If your child likes cheese**, make dishes like cheesy cauliflower and broccoli or macaroni and cheese with broccoli.

✳ **Instead of boring mashed potatoes**, mash some potato and carrot together with a little butter, milk, and seasoning.

✳ **Children often like stir-fries**, and you can pack these full of vegetables, such as finely sliced carrots and snow peas. Just stir in some noodles and teriyaki sauce.

✳ **Crunchy raw vegetables** are often more appealing than cooked vegetables. Try giving your child carrot and cucumber sticks and slices of sweet pepper with a tasty dip. If you are out and about, store them in small plastic bags to keep them from drying out.

✳ **If all else fails, disguise vegetables.** Blend them into a tomato sauce for pasta (see the hidden vegetable bolognaise recipe on pages 126–127). You could also try chopping vegetables

foods for fussy kids

My little girl of 18 months used to eat so well, but has recently become a fussy eater. Do you have any suggestions for what I can feed her?

Without going to unnecessary lengths, try to make your child's food not only taste good, but look good too. Make mini portions in ramekins, such as the Mini chicken pies (pages 160–161) and First fish pie (pages 120–121). Or try chicken skewers and threading bite-sized pieces of fruit on to a straw. You could also try making your own healthy versions of popular foods, like Muffin pizzas with hidden vegetable tomato sauce (pages 152–153) or fresh fruit popsicles (pages 174–175). I also find that kids really enjoy ethnic-style foods. Try making Nasi goreng (page 157) or Annabel's chicken enchiladas (pages 158–159).

ask annabel

tips

If your child is a fussy eater, encourage good behavior by praising him when he eats well or tries something new

Cooking with your children is a great way to get them to try new foods. Set a good example by making tasty, healthy foods

Do not give your child low-fat foods, such as skim milk or low-fat yogurt before the age of two

into small pieces and hiding them inside a wrap. Just cover with tomato sauce and grated cheese and brown under the broiler.

✳ **Remember that frozen vegetables** are as good as fresh. Try giving your child a mixture of frozen peas and sweet corn.

✳ **Don't give up on salad**. Make one with cucumber, cherry tomato, shredded iceberg lettuce, grated carrot, and sweet corn, and serve with a tasty dressing. Whisk together one tablespoon of balsamic vinegar, one tablespoon of soy sauce, a pinch each of caster (superfine) sugar and dried mustard, four tablespoons of light olive oil, and some freshly ground black pepper

✳ **Make a star chart**. Every time your child eats a new vegetable, put a star on the chart. When a whole line is filled with stars, reward him with a treat such as a trip to a theme park or a little toy.

● overweight children

At around the age of two or three, children can become overweight. Young children need plenty of nourishment, so unless your child is seriously overweight, don't take drastic measures. Your aim should be to keep your child's weight steady and as he grows, he will slim down. If you think your child is seriously overweight, however, you should

seek professional help. Obesity is becoming a huge problem across the world (see below). We need to reverse this trend and encourage our

global obesity crisis

✳ **It is estimated** that nearly one in five children in the United States is overweight.

✳ **Over the past three decades**, the childhood obesity rate in the United States has almost doubled for preschool children. Over 15 percent of American children are obese, and this number is climbing at an alarming rate.

✳ **Researchers estimate**, that by the year 2010, nearly half of the children in North America will be overweight.

✳ **Childhood obesity** can increase the risk for Type 2 diabetes, hypertension, heart disease, stroke, and can lead to sleep apnea.

✳ **Obesity affects many countries** of the world. Scientists predict that the number of overweight children will increase significantly over the next few years in Southeast Asia, the Middle East, and South America.

children to eat healthy and make good food choices from a young age. It can be difficult, especially when your child pesters you for unhealthy food; follow my strategies for encouraging healthy eating, below.

encouraging healthy eating

✳ **Start the day well**. It's not good for your child to go to day care on an empty stomach. Your child needs energy and concentration until lunch. Whole-grain cereals, such as oatmeal, release sugars slowly, avoiding the highs and lows of sugary refined cereals. Read labels carefully and check that the cereal contains less than ⅓oz (10g) of sugar per 3½oz (100g).

✳ **Set a good example**. You can't expect your child to eat well if you graze in front of the television and live off of junk food and take-out. It can take just 15 minutes to make a delicious meal for the whole family. Cook food from scratch so your child gets used to seeing you using a range of healthy ingredients. Eat meals together when possible, and don't let your child get into the habit of snacking in front of the television.

✳ **Don't pander to fussy eaters**. The more you give in to your child, offering only a few favorites like chicken nuggets, fries, and pizza, the more fussy your child will become.

✳ **Watch what you drink**. You can switch from full-fat to semi-skim milk once your child is two. It contains the same amount of calcium as full-fat milk. Make sure your child drinks enough water and limit juices.

● cook with your children

Most children love to cook, and a good way to get them to try new foods and to enjoy healthy meals is to encourage them to have a hand in preparing food. Children love to help with cracking eggs, kneading and rolling out dough, or mixing batters.

Cooking is a great way of bonding with your child, and it's educational too. He will learn lots of new skills such as counting, weighing, measuring, and telling the time.

Involve your child in making the recipes in this section. He can help spread the tomato sauce on to the muffins and make shapes with the cheese for the Muffin pizzas (pages 152–153), for example.

● the importance of exercise

All children need daily exercise, and although most toddlers and small children are on the go all day, some may need a little more persuasion to be active. Even if they need a little encouragement, it's worth getting your child into the habit of staying active as early as possible to make exercise part of their daily lives as they get older.

Get fit together—take your little one to the park and let him run around or take him on a walk around the block or to a playgroup. If you feel that your child is quite sedentary in his activities, try to replace quieter pastimes such as watching television or playing with toy bricks or dolls with more energetic ones, like playing tag in the backyard or dancing to music.

If your child is at a day care or with a babysitter while you're at work, find out how much exercise he is getting during the day. Make sure he has regular activity periods and space to run and play.

strategies that worked for me

Use this space to record the ways you encourage your little one to eat healthy—whether it's recipe ideas for sneaking vegetables into your child's diet, healthy snacks that your child enjoys, or strategies for dealing with your little fussy eater.

date first tried.....................................

reaction ....
....
....
....
....
....

what I thought ....
....
....

my variations ....
....
....
....
....
....
....
....
....

check
reaction

muffin pizza with hidden vegetable-tomato sauce

My children love these mini pizzas. They even eat them for breakfast sometimes! In this recipe, I have puréed the vegetables and tomatoes before cooking, because it is easier to blend when there is more liquid, and easier to tell when the sauce is thick enough.

- PREPARATION: 10 MINUTES
- COOKING: 30–35 MINUTES
- MAKES 1 PORTION
- PROVIDES PROTEIN, CALCIUM, BETA-CAROTENE, VITS C & D, PREBIOTICS
- SAUCE SUITABLE FOR FREEZING

1 large shallot, finely chopped

½ small leek, thinly sliced

1 small carrot, peeled and grated

¼ zucchini, grated

1 tbsp olive oil

1 small clove garlic, crushed

2 tbsp tomato paste

2 sun-dried tomatoes in oil, drained

2 tbsp ketchup

1 (14oz/400g) can crushed tomatoes

1½ tsp sugar

Salt and pepper

1 English muffin, split in half

¼ cup shredded Cheddar or mozzarella cheese

Put the vegetables in a large saucepan with the oil and sauté them until soft but not colored, 8–10 minutes. Add the garlic and cook for 1 minute longer. Transfer to a blender. Add the tomato paste, sun-dried tomatoes, ketchup, canned tomatoes, and sugar, and process until smooth. Return to the pan and simmer, stirring occasionally, until thick, about 20 minutes. Season with salt and pepper, then let cool slightly.

Preheat the broiler. Arrange the muffin halves, cut side up, on a baking sheet. Spread 1 tbsp of sauce on each muffin and scatter the cheese on top (or arrange in a pattern). Broil 2–3in (5–7cm) from the heat, until the cheese is melted and bubbling, 2–3 minutes. Let cool slightly, then cut into strips or squares to serve. For older children, you can leave the muffin halves whole or cut them in half.

Note: There will be lots of leftover sauce, but it freezes very well, for up to 3 months. Freeze in individual portions so that you can thaw it quickly. This also makes a delicious sauce for pasta and it's a good way to get children to eat more vegetables, because what they can't see, they can't pick out. For a pasta sauce, cut down the cooking time so the sauce is not as thick.

date first tried ....

reaction ....

what I thought ....

my variations ....

check
reaction

chicken balls with spaghetti and tomato sauce

Chicken balls flavored with apple are a signature dish of mine. Lots of moms tell me how popular they are with their children. Delicious with spaghetti and tomato sauce, they can also be served as finger food. If you are freezing this, freeze the chicken balls and tomato sauce separately in individual portions and then cook the spaghetti fresh.

- PREPARATION: 25 MINUTES
- COOKING: 20 MINUTES
- MAKES 5–6 PORTIONS
- PROVIDES PROTEIN, IRON, SELENIUM, ZINC, CALCIUM, BETA-CAROTENE, FOLATE, VIT D, PREBIOTICS
- SUITABLE FOR FREEZING

Tomato sauce

1–2 tbsp olive oil

2 onions, finely chopped

1 clove garlic, crushed

1 (14oz/400g) can crushed tomatoes

1 tbsp tomato paste

2 tsp sugar

¼ tsp dried oregano

Chicken balls

1 cup ground chicken

1 small apple, peeled and grated

1 tsp fresh thyme leaves

¼ cup freshly grated Parmesan cheese

½ cup fresh white bread crumbs

Salt and pepper

All-purpose flour to dust hands

3 tbsp sunflower oil, for frying

To serve

About 1oz (30g) spaghetti per portion

Chopped fresh parsley or basil

Heat the oil in a saucepan and gently cook the onions until softened, about 10 minutes. Spoon half the onions into a bowl and let cool (these will be used for the chicken balls). Add the garlic to the onions left in the pan and sauté for 1 minute longer, then add all the remaining sauce ingredients plus ½ cup water. Cover and simmer for 7–8 minutes, stirring occasionally.

Meanwhile, to make the chicken balls, add the ground chicken, grated apple, thyme, and Parmesan to the onions in the bowl. Add the bread crumbs and season with salt and pepper. Mix together well. With floured hands, form teaspoons of the mixture into about 20–24 small balls. Heat the sunflower oil in a frying pan and brown the balls all over. Transfer the balls to the pan of tomato sauce and simmer, uncovered, for 8–10 minutes.

Cook the spaghetti according to the directions on the package. Drain and toss with the chicken balls and sauce. Sprinkle with a little parsley or basil.

"Try making these with ground turkey or beef as a tasty alternative to chicken"

date first tried ....

reaction ....

what I thought ....

my variations ....

check
reaction

pasta salad with pesto dressing

I have made two different dressings to go with this salad. The first one uses mayonnaise, and is a bit creamier. If you are taking this salad out with you, then you might prefer to use the second dressing made with olive oil and some of the less perishable add-ins.

- PREPARATION: 10 MINUTES
- COOKING: 12 MINUTES
- MAKES 2 PORTIONS
- PROVIDES PROTEIN, CALCIUM, IRON, BETA-CAROTENE, FOLATE, VITS A, B_1, B_3, C, & D, PREBIOTICS

2oz (55g) pasta spirals (about ⅓ cup)

Dressing 1

1½ tbsp mayonnaise

1½ tbsp pesto

3–4 drops of lemon juice

Dressing 2

1 tbsp olive oil

2 tsp pesto

3–4 drops of lemon juice

Add-ins

⅓ cup shredded cooked chicken (see page 96)

⅓ cup cubed Cheddar cheese

¼ cup cooked ham, cut into thin strips

1 medium tomato, seeded and cut into strips

1 scallion, thinly sliced

¼ red or orange bell pepper, cut into strips

Small handful of cooked broccoli florets

¾in (2cm) piece of cucumber, cut into matchsticks

Cook the pasta according to package directions. Meanwhile, mix together the ingredients for dressing 1 or 2. Drain the pasta and rinse well with cold water, then toss in the dressing. Mix in two or three add-ins of your choice. Keep the salad in the refrigerator until needed.

nasi goreng

A delicious Indonesian recipe.

- PREPARATION: 15 MINUTES
- COOKING: 15 MINUTES
- MAKES 4 PORTIONS
- PROVIDES PROTEIN, IRON, MAGNESIUM, ZINC, VITS A, D, & E, PREBIOTICS

1 skinless, boneless chicken breast half, diced

$2/3$ cup long-grain rice

$1\frac{1}{2}$ tbsp vegetable oil

1 tsp toasted sesame oil

2 shallots or 1 onion, finely chopped

1 small clove garlic, crushed

$\frac{1}{2}$ small red bell pepper, finely chopped

$\frac{1}{2}$ tbsp chopped fresh parsley

$\frac{1}{2}$ tbsp mild curry powder

$\frac{1}{4}$ tsp turmeric

Small pinch of mild chili powder

$\frac{1}{4}$ cup chicken stock

$1/3$ cup frozen green peas

2 small scallions, finely sliced

$\frac{1}{2}$ tbsp dark brown sugar

$\frac{1}{4}$ cup finely chopped roasted peanuts

Marinade

$1\frac{1}{2}$ tbsp soy sauce

1 tsp toasted sesame oil

$\frac{1}{2}$ tbsp dark brown sugar

Omelet

1 egg

$\frac{1}{4}$ tsp sugar

Small pinch of salt

1 tsp sunflower oil

date first tried ......

reaction ......

what I thought ......

my variations ......

check reaction

Marinate the chicken in the soy sauce, sesame oil, and sugar for 30 minutes, then drain, reserving the marinade. While the chicken is marinating, cook the rice according to the package directions.

To make the omelet, beat together the egg, sugar, salt, and $\frac{1}{2}$ tsp cold water. Heat the oil in a small nonstick frying pan. Pour in the egg mixture and swirl to cover the bottom of the pan in a thin layer. Cook for about 1 minute until set, then turn over and cook for 30 seconds on the other side. Remove the omelet from the pan and cut into strips. Set aside.

Heat the oils in a wok or frying pan and sauté the shallots for 3 minutes. Add the garlic and cook for 30 seconds. Add the red pepper and sauté for 2 minutes, then add the parsley and chicken. Cook for 3 minutes. Stir in the curry powder, turmeric, and chili powder with the reserved marinade and the stock. Cook for 1 minute. Add the peas and scallions and cook for 2 minutes. Stir in the rice, sugar, peanuts, and omelet, and heat through.

Note: Keep leftovers in the refrigerator for up to 24 hours. Add $\frac{1}{2}$ tsp water and microwave until piping hot, 1–2 minutes. Cool slightly before serving.

date first tried ....

reaction ....
....
....
....
....

what I thought ....
....
....
....

my variations ....
....
....
....
....
....
....

check
reaction

annabel's chicken enchiladas

Wraps are the new trendy food and are very popular with children. An enchilada is a Mexican wrap—a flour tortilla rolled around a filling, covered with a sauce and grated cheese, and baked. It's a great way to sneak some extra veggies into the diet. All my children love it.

- PREPARATION: 25–30 MINUTES
- COOKING: 45 MINUTES
- MAKES 8 ENCHILADAS
- PROVIDES PROTEIN, IRON, SELENIUM, ZINC, CALCIUM, FOLATE, VITS A, C, & D, PREBIOTICS
- SUITABLE FOR FREEZING

8 small flour tortilla wraps

Tomato sauce

1 tbsp olive oil

1 red onion, finely chopped

1 clove garlic, crushed

½ tsp dried oregano

1 (14oz/400g) can crushed tomatoes

1 tbsp tomato paste

1 tbsp minced sun-dried tomatoes in oil (drained)

1 tsp sugar

Chicken filling

1 tbsp olive oil

1 clove garlic, crushed

1 red onion, chopped

1 red bell pepper, seeded and diced

1 small zucchini, diced

1½ cups ground chicken

2 cups shredded Cheddar cheese

To make the sauce, heat the oil in a large saucepan and sauté the onion until soft, about 5 minutes. Add the garlic and cook for 1 minute, then add the remaining sauce ingredients. Bring to a boil and simmer until thick, about 20 minutes, stirring occasionally. Season and blend until smooth.

Make the chicken filling while the sauce is simmering. Heat the olive oil in a large frying pan or wok and stir in the garlic, onion, red pepper, and zucchini. Cook for 5 minutes, then add the chicken and season with salt and pepper. Continue to cook, stirring occasionally, until the chicken is cooked through, 7–8 minutes. Stir in half of the cheese until melted.

Preheat the oven to 400°F (200°C). Lightly oil a large baking dish.

Warm the tortillas slightly (in the oven or microwave), then divide the filling among them, spooning it down the center. Roll up the tortillas and arrange, seam side down and in one layer, in the dish. Spoon the sauce on top and sprinkle with the remaining cheese. Bake until the cheese is bubbling and golden brown, 15–20 minutes. Cool to warm before serving.

Note: Freeze (in individual portions) unbaked, without the cheese; thaw overnight in the refrigerator, then add the cheese before baking.

date first tried

reaction

what I thought

my variations

check
reaction

mini chicken pies

Sweating the vegetables slowly with thyme and then reducing the white wine vinegar gives a lovely flavor to the filling for these pies. If you cut the chicken across the grain into thin slices, it breaks up the fibers and helps make the chicken very tender. The pies freeze well, so you can bake and serve one, then freeze the other three. Or bake in larger dishes to feed the whole family.

● PREPARATION: 25–30 MINUTES
● COOKING: 30–35 MINUTES
● MAKES 4 INDIVIDUAL PIES
● PROVIDES PROTEIN, IRON, POTASSIUM, ZINC, BETA-CAROTENE, VITS D & E
● SUITABLE FOR FREEZING

3 tbsp butter

1 small shallot, diced

1 medium carrot, peeled and diced

½ small leek, thinly sliced

¼ tsp chopped fresh thyme leaves

4 tsp white wine vinegar

2½ tbsp cornstarch

1¾ cups hot chicken stock

2 tbsp crème fraîche

Salt and pepper

1lb (450g) potatoes, peeled and cubed (about 3½ cups)

3 tbsp milk

8oz (225g) skinless, boneless chicken breast, cut into thin, bite-size slices

1 egg white, lightly beaten (optional)

Melt 2 tbsp of the butter and sweat the vegetables with the thyme until soft, about 10 minutes. Add the vinegar and boil until it has evaporated. Stir in the cornstarch, then add the stock a little at a time, stirring, to make a smooth sauce. Add the crème fraîche and season to taste with salt and pepper. Let the sauce cool.

Cook the potatoes in plenty of boiling water until just tender, about 15 minutes. Drain the potatoes, then mash them well. Beat in the remaining butter and the milk, and season to taste.

Divide the chicken among four ramekins or small ovenproof dishes (I use ramekins about 4in/10cm in diameter) and spoon the sauce on top. Cover with the potato mash and use a fork to mark the surface with lines.

Preheat the oven to 400°F (200°C). Put the dish(es) on a baking sheet and bake for 30 minutes. If the pies have come straight from the refrigerator, bake for an extra 5 minutes. The tops can be browned further under the broiler—if you brush them with a little egg white, they will brown nicely.

Note: To freeze, wrap the unbaked potato-topped pies well; thaw overnight in the refrigerator before baking.

teriyaki salmon

Eating food on a stick is always more fun than using a fork or spoon (although for small children, it is safer to remove the salmon from the skewers to serve), and this is a tasty way to get your child to eat more oily fish. The cooked skewers can be kept in the refrigerator for up to two days, and taste just as good cold.

- PREPARATION: 10 MINUTES, PLUS 30 MINUTES TO SOAK SKEWERS
- COOKING: 6 MINUTES
- MAKES 6 PORTIONS
- PROVIDES PROTEIN, OMEGA-3s, IRON, VITS D & E, SELENIUM

1 tbsp sesame seeds

1 piece of skinless, boneless salmon fillet weighing about 7oz (200g)

¼ tsp grated fresh ginger

1 tbsp clear honey

1½ tsp soy sauce

Put six small wooden skewers in cold water to soak for 30 minutes. Meanwhile, toast the sesame seeds in a small frying pan over medium heat for 2–3 minutes, stirring two or three times. Spread out on a plate to cool.

Preheat the broiler. Cut the salmon into ½in (1.25cm) cubes. Thread three or four cubes onto each soaked skewer and lay the skewers in one layer on a foil-lined baking sheet.

Mix the ginger with the honey and soy sauce to make the teriyaki sauce. Brush some of this sauce onto the salmon and broil, 2–3in (5–7cm) from the heat, for 2 minutes. Brush the salmon again with the teriyaki sauce and broil for 2 minutes longer. Turn the skewers over and repeat the brushing and broiling process.

Sprinkle the sesame seeds over the salmon before serving.

Variation: Add 1 tsp sweet chili sauce to the teriyaki sauce.

date first tried

reaction

what I thought

my variations

check reaction

> Try to include oily fish in your child's diet twice a week. Other good ways to serve it are in fish pies or fishcakes

date first tried.................................

reaction ....

....

....

what I thought ....

....

....

my variations ....

....

....

....

....

....

check
reaction

my first sweet and sour pork

Small children will find ground pork a little easier to eat than cubes, and they often don't notice the vegetables in this! Serve with rice.

- PREPARATION: 10 MINUTES
- COOKING: 8 MINUTES
- MAKES 2 PORTIONS
- PROVIDES PROTEIN, IRON, SELENIUM, MANGANESE, ZINC, FOLATE, VITS A, B_3, & C, PREBIOTICS
- SUITABLE FOR FREEZING

2 tbsp ketchup

1½ tsp soy sauce

2 tbsp pineapple juice (from the can)

1 tsp cornstarch

1 tbsp sunflower oil

½ cup ground pork (or chicken)

2 scallions, thinly sliced

¼ red bell pepper, diced

1 canned pineapple ring, diced

2 tbsp canned corn, drained

Mix together the ketchup, soy sauce, pineapple juice, cornstarch, and 4 tbsp water in a small bowl. Set this sauce mixture aside.

Heat the sunflower oil in a wok and stir-fry the pork for 3 minutes, breaking it up well as you cook. Add the scallions and red pepper, and cook until the vegetables are soft and the pork is browned, about 3 minutes longer. Add the pineapple, corn, and sauce mixture and cook until the sauce is bubbling and thickened, about 1–2 minutes.

egg fried rice with chicken and shrimp

Children like egg fried rice. You can make it with other vegetables like diced steamed carrots, or leave out the shrimp and add extra chicken.

- PREPARATION: 15 MINUTES, PLUS
  30 MINUTES MARINATING
- COOKING: 8 MINUTES
- MAKES 4 PORTIONS
- PROVIDES PROTEIN, IRON, SELENIUM,
  ZINC, FOLATE, VITS A, D, & E, PREBIOTICS

5oz (150g) skinless, boneless chicken, cut into small cubes (about ⅔ cup)

1 cup basmati rice

2 tbsp sunflower oil

1 small onion, finely chopped

⅓ heaping cup frozen green peas

1 large scallion, finely sliced

4oz (115g) peeled, cooked small shrimp (about ½ cup)

Marinade

1 tbsp soy sauce

½ tsp sugar

1 tsp cornstarch

Omelet

1 tsp sunflower oil

1 extra large egg, beaten with a pinch of salt

Mix together the marinade ingredients and marinate the chicken for at least 30 minutes. Meanwhile, cook the rice according to the package directions.

To make the omelet, heat the oil in a small frying pan. Add the beaten egg and tilt the pan so that the egg covers the bottom thinly. Cook until set. Transfer to a cutting board, roll up, and cut into strips. Set aside.

Heat the 2 tbsp oil in a wok and sauté the onion for 2 minutes. Add the chicken with its marinade and sauté for 2 more minutes. Add the frozen peas, scallion, and shrimp, and cook for 1 minute. Fluff up the rice with a fork, add to the wok with the omelet strips, and stir-fry for 1 minute.

Note: Leftovers can be kept, well wrapped, in the refrigerator for up to 24 hours. Add ½ tsp water and microwave until piping hot, 1–2 minutes. Cool slightly before serving.

date first tried

reaction

what I thought

my variations

check
reaction

date first tried

reaction

what I thought

my variations

check
reaction

thai-style chicken with noodles

I find that most children love noodles, and you will be able to sneak in some veggies with them. Feel free to make up your own version using vegetables of your choice—mini broccoli florets work well. It's fun to serve this in a bowl and let your child try eating this using child-friendly chopsticks, which are joined at the top.

- PREPARATION: 15–20 MINUTES, PLUS 1 HOUR MARINATING
- COOKING: 8–10 MINUTES
- MAKES 4–6 PORTIONS
- PROVIDES PROTEIN, IRON, SELENIUM, ZINC, BETA-CAROTENE, FOLATE, VITS B_2 & C, PREBIOTICS
- SUITABLE FOR FREEZING

1 tsp fish sauce

½ tsp soy sauce

½ tsp sugar

8oz (225g) skinless, boneless chicken breast, cut into small strips

4oz (115g) egg noodles

3 tsp sunflower oil

1 small clove garlic, crushed

½ tsp grated fresh ginger

¼ cup thinly sliced shallot

1½ tsp mild curry paste

1 small carrot, peeled and cut into matchsticks

Small handful of snow peas, cut into matchsticks

¼ red bell pepper, cut into matchsticks

½ cup chicken stock

1 cup coconut milk

1 tsp lime juice

Salt and pepper (optional)

Mix together the fish sauce, soy sauce, and sugar in a medium bowl, stirring until the sugar has dissolved. Add the chicken and toss to coat. Let marinate for 1 hour. Meanwhile, cook the noodles according to package directions; rinse with cold water and drain well. Toss with 1 tsp of the oil.

Heat the remaining oil in a wok. Add the garlic, ginger, and shallot, and stir-fry for 1 minute. Add the chicken with its marinade and stir-fry until the chicken is almost cooked, 3–4 minutes. Mix in the curry paste followed by the vegetables, chicken stock, and coconut milk. Bring to a boil, then reduce the heat and simmer until the vegetables are tender and the chicken is thoroughly cooked, about 5 minutes.

Add the noodles and toss in the sauce for 1–2 minutes to reheat. Add the lime juice and season, if desired, with a little salt and pepper.

Note: Leftovers can be kept in the refrigerator for up to 2 days; reheat in the microwave (adding 1 tsp water per portion) until piping hot, 1–2 minutes. If frozen, thaw in the refrigerator overnight before reheating.

date first tried..........................

reaction..........................

what I thought..........................

my variations..........................

check
reaction

meatloaf with tangy bbq sauce

This is a moist and tender meatloaf. I have mixed the ingredients in a food processor to give a finer texture, which small children tend to prefer. However, you could just mix everything together in a bowl. With a "free-form" meatloaf, the yummy sauce can be brushed all over.

- PREPARATION: 15 MINUTES
- COOKING: 45 MINUTES
- MAKES 6 PORTIONS
- PROVIDES PROTEIN, IRON, SELENIUM, ZINC, VIT C, PREBIOTICS
- SUITABLE FOR FREEZING

Sauce

½ cup ketchup

2 tbsp maple syrup or clear honey

1 tsp soy sauce

1 tsp Worcestershire sauce

1 tsp balsamic vinegar

2 tbsp orange juice

Meatloaf

⅔ cup fresh white bread crumbs

6 tbsp milk

1 small red onion, finely diced

2 tsp olive oil

1 clove garlic, crushed

8oz (225g) ground beef or a mixture of beef and pork (about 1 cup)

¼ tsp dried oregano

Salt and pepper

Preheat the oven to 350°F (180°C).

Mix the ketchup, maple syrup (or honey), soy sauce, Worcestershire sauce, and balsamic vinegar together in a medium saucepan. Transfer 3 tbsp of this mixture to a bowl, then add the orange juice to the saucepan. Set aside.

Mix the bread crumbs and milk in another bowl and let soak for 10 minutes. Meanwhile, sauté the onion in the oil for 5 minutes until translucent. Add the garlic and cook for 1 minute longer. Transfer to a food processor and add the bread crumbs, beef, oregano, and 2 tbsp of the sauce in the bowl. Season with salt and pepper, then process until well-combined.

Spoon the mixture onto a baking sheet lined with parchment paper and pat into a loaf shape roughly 8in (20cm) long and just over 3in (7cm) wide. Bake for 20 minutes. Brush with half of the sauce left in the bowl and with any juices. Bake for 20 minutes longer, then brush with the remaining sauce from the bowl. Bake for a final 5 minutes.

Rest for 10 minutes before slicing (cut into bite-size cubes for toddlers). Heat the sauce left in the pan until bubbling, to serve with the meatloaf.

Note: Freeze individual slices with sauce on top; thaw overnight in the refrigerator, then reheat in the microwave for 45–60 seconds.

cute cottage pies

Most children like grated carrots, but if your baby is particularly fussy about vegetables, then sauté the carrot with the other vegetables and blend into the sauce. For younger babies, it might be a good idea to transfer the cooked ground beef to a food processor and blend for a few seconds to get a finer texture before adding it to the cooked vegetables.

- PREPARATION: 20 MINUTES
- COOKING: 20–25 MINUTES
- MAKES 4–6 INDIVIDUAL PIES
- PROVIDES PROTEIN, IRON, SELENIUM, ZINC, POTASSIUM, CALCIUM, BETA-CAROTENE, VITS C & D
- SUITABLE FOR FREEZING

3 tbsp olive oil

8oz (225g) lean ground beef (about 1 cup)

½ medium onion, chopped

½ medium leek, sliced

1 cup diced cremini mushrooms

2 sprigs of fresh thyme, leaves only

1 cup beef stock

2 tsp tomato paste

1 tbsp soy sauce

1 tsp Worcestershire sauce

1 medium carrot, peeled and coarsely grated

1lb (450g) potatoes, peeled and cubed (about 3½ cups)

1 tbsp butter

3 tbsp milk

Salt and pepper

4–6 tbsp shredded Cheddar cheese

Heat 1 tbsp olive oil in a large nonstick frying pan and stir-fry the beef until well-browned and crumbly, 5–7 minutes. Transfer to a bowl and set aside.

Add the remaining olive oil to the pan and sauté the onion, leek, and mushrooms with the thyme until soft, 7–8 minutes. Add the beef stock, then transfer to a blender and blend until smooth. Return to the frying pan along with the beef, and stir in the tomato paste, soy sauce, Worcestershire sauce, and carrots. Bring to a boil, then lower the heat and simmer for 10 minutes. Divide among four to six small baking dishes or ramekins.

While the beef is simmering, cook the potatoes in boiling water until just tender, about 15 minutes. Drain, then mash well. Beat in the butter and milk and season to taste. Spoon the potato over the beef filling and use a fork to make decorative lines on the surface. Sprinkle with the cheese.

Preheat the oven to 400°F (200°C). Set the dish(es) on a baking sheet and bake until hot in the center and golden on top, about 20 minutes. If the pies have come straight from the refrigerator, bake for an extra 5 minutes. The tops can be browned further under the broiler, if desired.

Note: If freezing the pies, thaw overnight in the refrigerator before baking.

date first tried

reaction

what I thought

my variations

check reaction

date first tried...............................

reaction...

....

....

....

....

what I thought ....

....

....

my variations ....

....

....

....

....

....

....

....

check
reaction

moroccan lamb

Here's a great recipe for batch cooking. Serve with couscous or rice.

- PREPARATION: 25 MINUTES
- COOKING: 1¾ HOURS
- MAKES 8–10 PORTIONS
- PROVIDES PROTEIN, IRON, SELENIUM, ZINC, VITS A, B$_3$, & C, PREBIOTICS
- SUITABLE FOR FREEZING

1lb (450g) boned leg of lamb, cubed

2 tbsp all-purpose flour

Salt and pepper

2–3 tbsp sunflower oil

1 large onion, chopped

1 large clove garlic, crushed

1¼ tsp ground cinnamon

1½ tsp mild curry paste

2½ cups vegetable stock

1 (14oz/400g) can crushed tomatoes

5 tbsp tomato paste

1 tbsp mango chutney

½ sweet apple, grated

1 cup chopped dried apricots

Toss the lamb cubes in seasoned flour. Heat the oil in a medium Dutch oven (or use a heavy-bottomed saucepan with a tight-fitting lid) and brown the lamb all over. Remove the lamb and set aside.

Add the onion to the pot and fry until soft, 7–8 minutes. Add the garlic, cinnamon, and curry paste and cook for 1 minute, then add any leftover flour and cook for 2 minutes. Remove from the heat and stir in the stock, a little at a time. Return the lamb to the casserole and stir in the tomatoes, tomato paste, mango chutney, and apple. Season to taste.

Set the pot over medium heat and bring to a simmer. Cover and cook very gently for 1 hour, stirring occasionally. Add the apricots and continue to cook, uncovered, until the lamb is tender, about 30–45 minutes longer.

mini croque monsieur

This is a generous portion for an 18-month-old, but good for older babies. The trick to these gourmet ham and cheese sandwiches is to roll out the bread slices thinly so that the sandwich is crispy and not too thick for small mouths. You can make variations, such as substituting smoked turkey or chicken for the ham, using just cheese (double the quantity), or spreading a little ketchup and butter on the bread before adding the ham. Instead of toasting under the broiler, you can cook the sandwich in a preheated nonstick frying pan over medium heat.

- PREPARATION: 5 MINUTES
- COOKING: ABOUT 4 MINUTES
- MAKES 1 PORTION
- PROVIDES PROTEIN, IRON, SELENIUM, ZINC, CALCIUM

2 slices bread

1 slice cooked ham

¼ cup shredded Cheddar cheese

1 tbsp butter, at room temperature

Preheat the broiler.

Use a rolling pin to roll out the slices of bread so that they are nice and thin. Lay the ham on one slice of bread and scatter the cheese on top. Cover with the second slice of bread. Spread the butter in a thin layer over the outside on both sides of the sandwich, making sure you go right to the edges.

Toast the sandwich under the broiler, 2–3in (5–7cm) from the heat, until the bread is golden and the cheese has melted, about 2 minutes on each side. Let cool slightly, then cut into fingers.

Variation: Try making ham and cheese quesadillas too. Sprinkle grated cheese onto a tortilla, cover with a layer of sliced ham, and sprinkle a little more cheese on top. Cover with another tortilla, and cook for 1½ minutes on each side in a dry frying pan. Cut into slices to serve.

date first tried

reaction

what I thought

my variations

check reaction

" Kids will love these ham and cheese grilled sandwiches. Try them with chicken or turkey, or the delicious quesadilla variation too "

date first tried.................................

reaction...

....

....

....

....

what I thought ....

....

....

....

my variations ....

....

....

....

....

....

....

....

check
reaction

apple and blackberry surprise

This is very tasty, and a bit like a luxury oatmeal with caramelized apples and blackberries. You could halve the quantities to make enough for two children, but I'd stick to four so you can have some too!

- PREPARATION: 20 MINUTES
- COOKING: 20 MINUTES
- MAKES 4 PORTIONS
- PROVIDES CALCIUM, FOLATE, VITS A, B_1, B_2, B_3, C, & D, PREBIOTICS

4 tbsp butter

1 cup rolled oats

¼ cup sugar

2 Granny Smith apples, peeled, cored, and sliced

⅔ cup heavy cream

½ cup thick (Greek-style) plain yogurt

2 tbsp clear honey

2 tbsp light brown sugar

1 heaping cup blackberries

Melt half the butter in a small pan, add the oats, and cook for 1 minute. Stir in half the sugar and cook, stirring, until the oats are lightly caramelized, about 4–5 minutes. Transfer to a baking sheet, spread out, and let cool.

Melt the remaining butter in a large pan and sauté the apple slices until they begin to soften, 3–4 minutes. Add the remaining sugar and cook until caramelized, 8–10 minutes longer. Let cool.

Lightly whip the cream, then fold in the yogurt, honey, brown sugar, and oats. Reserve eight blackberries; stir the rest into the yogurt cream, crushing them slightly. Layer the blackberry cream and the apples in four glasses and top with the reserved blackberries.

date first tried ....

reaction ....

what I thought ....

my variations ....

check reaction

red fruit rocket popsicles

It's so easy to make your own yummy fruit popsicles. The amount of sugar you add will depend on how sweet the fruit is. If your berries and watermelon are very sweet, you can reduce the sugar by 1 tbsp.

- PREPARATION: 10 MINUTES, PLUS FREEZING
- COOKING: NONE
- MAKES ABOUT 1¾ CUPS
- PROVIDES POTASSIUM, BETA-CAROTENE, FOLATE, VITS B_6 & C

1 heaping cup strawberries, halved

2 cups raspberries

1 cup diced watermelon, seeded

¼ cup sugar

Blend all the ingredients together until smooth. Taste for sweetness and add a little extra sugar if needed. Strain the mixture to remove the berry seeds, then spoon or pour into rocket-shaped popsicle molds and freeze.

mango and pineapple tropical popsicles

Popsicles are always a good way to get children to eat fruit. For this recipe, be sure to use a very ripe mango.

- PREPARATION: 10 MINUTES, PLUS FREEZING
- COOKING: NONE
- MAKES ABOUT 2 CUPS
- PROVIDES MANGANESE, BETA-CAROTENE, FOLATE, VITS B_3 & C

1 cup canned pineapple (rings or chunks), with juice

1 large ripe mango, peeled and pitted

¼ cup confectioners' (powdered) sugar

1 tbsp coconut milk

1 tsp lime juice (or lemon)

Blend everything together until smooth. Spoon or pour into popsicle molds and freeze.

date first tried ....

reaction ....

what I thought ....

my variations ....

check reaction

"One way to get your child to eat more fruit is to make fresh fruit popsicles. You can also freeze store-bought fruit smoothies or juices"

meal planner: healthy habits

This meal planner provides suggestions for your toddler's meals, many of which are drawn from this book. Either use the planner pages to map out your toddler's meals for the next weeks or to keep a record of your child's diet week-by-week.

breakfast	lunch	dinner	extras
wheat-based cereal yogurt fruit	Mini chicken pies (pp160–161) with broccoli Orchard crisp (p130)	Teriyaki salmon (pp162–163) with rice or vegetables fruit	rice cakes dried fruit yogurt
scrambled egg on whole-grain toast	My first sweet and sour pork (p164) Orchard crisp (p130)	Egg fried rice with chicken and shrimp (p165) fruit	Mini croque monsieur (p171) fruit
oatmeal with honey fruit	Moroccan lamb (p170) with couscous My favorite frozen yogurt (p134); fruit	Muffin pizza (pp152–153) Apple and blackberry surprise (pp172–173)	carrot and cucumber sticks with a dip, e.g., hummus yogurt
fruit smoothie cereal yogurt or dried fruit	Chicken balls with spaghetti and tomato sauce (pp154–155) fruit	Stuffed baked potato with cheese and ham filling; Mango and pineapple popsicle (pp174–175)	cheese and grapes Ginger cookie shapes (p129)
boiled egg with fingers of toast fruit	Goujons of fish (p115) with oven-baked fries Red fruit rocket popsicle (pp174–175)	Annabel's chicken enchiladas (pp158–159) fruit	Finger food sandwiches (p90–92) Ginger cookie shapes (p129); fruit
granola with yogurt, honey, and fruit	Pasta salad with pesto dressing (p156) fruit	Cute cottage pies (p169) My favorite frozen yogurt (p134) fruit	grilled cheese on toast yogurt fruit
pancakes or waffles with maple syrup berries	Thai-style chicken with noodles (pp166–167) fruit	Meatloaf with tangy BBQ sauce (p168) Bananas "Foster" (p131)	Mini oatmeal-raisin cookies (pp102–103) yogurt fruit

● hidden vegetables

Sometimes you need to be inventive to encourage your child to eat vegetables. My first sweet and sour pork (page 164) is full of such lively flavors he may not spot the vegetables.

WEEK 1	breakfast	lunch	dinner	extras
day 1				
day 2				
day 3				
day 4				
day 5				
day 6				
day 7				

meal planner: weeks 2 and 3

Use these planners to record the meals you give your toddler over the following weeks. If you want to record your child's meals for longer than three weeks, simply photocopy this page. Pieces of fruit or yogurt make good snacks and desserts.

WEEK 2	breakfast	lunch	dinner	extras
day 1				
day 2				
day 3				
day 4				
day 5				
day 6				
day 7				

● eating with the family

Set a good example for your child by making delicious, healthy home-cooked meals that the whole family can enjoy. Take time to eat together as a family as often as you can.

WEEK 3	breakfast	lunch	dinner	extras
day 1				
day 2				
day 3				
day 4				
day 5				
day 6				
day 7				

other favorites

Use this page to write down your other favorite recipes, ideas for healthy and energy-boosting snacks, or recipe recommendations from your friends and family. It will be much easier to include your child in family meals, so enjoy experimenting!

foods my child loves and hates

Children have preferences from a young age. If your child rejects a food, try it again in a few weeks, in a totally different recipe.

Use this page to record your child's likes and dislikes. It will be amusing to look back on in years to come.

notes for growing up

Just because your little one has reached the age of three, doesn't mean you need to stop recording. Use this space to write down anything from your child's food likes and dislikes and food fads to favorite recipes and foods you cook together.

useful addresses

American Academy of Allergy Asthma & Immunology
555 East Wells Street
Milwaukee, WI 53202
Tel: (414) 272-6071
Web site: www.aaaai.org
A national organization dealing with allergy and related disorders. The website provides information on these disorders and a physician referral directory. The National Allergy Bureau ™ of the AAAAI's Aeroallergen Network reports pollen and mold spore levels to the public.

American Academy of Pediatrics
141 Northwest Point Boulevard
Elk Grove Village, IL 60007
Tel: (847)228-5005
www.aap.org
The primary professional association of pediatricians in the US. The web site provides in-depth information for parents on a wide range of medical and health topics.

American Dietetic Association
120 South Riverside Plaza
Chicago, IL 60606
Tel: (800) 877-1600
www.eatright.org
The world's largest organization of food and nutrition professionals. The web site includes nutritional fact sheets, and links to the new food pyramid and to the ADA Journal, available online by subscription.

American Vegan Society
56 Dinshah Lane, PO Box 369
Malaga, NJ 08328
Tel: (856) 694-2887
www.americanvegan.org
Provides useful advice on nutrition, and bringing up vegan children.

Annabel Karmel
49 Berkeley Square
London W1J 5AZ
Tel: (011 44 207) 355-4555
www.annabelkarmel.com
Annabel's web site includes advice on weaning, recipes, and a forum to discuss issues with other parents and caregivers. Purchase Annabel's other books online too.

Centers for Disease Control
1600 Clifton Road
Atlanta, GA 30333
Tel: (800) 311-3435
www.cdc.gov

Center for Science in the Public Interest
US office:
1875 Connecticut Avenue, NW
Washington, DC 20009
Tel: (202) 332-9110
Canadian office:
Suite 4550, CTTC Building
Ottawa, Ont. K1S 5R1
Tel: (613) 244-7337
www.cspinet.org
A consumer-advocacy organization that conducts research and advocacy in health and nutrition, and provide health and well-being information.

KidsHealth
www.kidshealth.com
Accurate, up-to-date, health information, including guidance on nutrition and feeding of infants and toddlers. Includes health and medical information for parents, topics of interest to teenagers, and content specifically for children.

La Leche League International

957 N. Plum Grove Road
Schaumburg, IL 60173
Tel: (800) 525-3243
www.llli.org
An organization founded to provide information and support to breastfeeding mothers. The web site covers a broad range of issues. Specific breastfeeding questions can be submitted online or directed to local La Leche League Leaders; chapters exist throughout the US, the provinces of Canada (www.lllc.ca), and around the world, and many local chapters have their own web sites. An interactive map helps the user find the nearest experts.

Nemours

4600 Touchton Road East
Building 200, Suite 500
Jacksonville, FL 32246
Tel: (904) 232-4100
www.nemours.org
Dedicated to providing quality healthcare for children through dissemination of information to the public (including the award-winning KidsHealth web site) and to the medical profession, and by pediatric medical centers in Florida and Delaware.

North American Vegetarian Society

PO Box 72
Dolgeville, NY 13329
Tel: (518) 568-7970
www.navs-online.org
Offers expert advice on nutritional issues and provides advice on recipes, approved products, and eating out. The web site includes lists of local contacts and links to independent affiliates through the US and Canada.

Produce for Better Health Foundation

www.5aday.com
www.fruitsandveggiesmore
matters.org
FoodChamps.org
Has three web sites geared toward parents and children.

Produce Marketing Association

1500 Casho Mill Road
Newark, DE 19714
Tel: (302) 738-7100
www.pma.com
The leading international trade organization for the entire produce and related products and services. The web site provides information for parents, children, and teachers.

The Food Allergy & Anaphylaxis Network

11781 Lee Jackson Highway
Fairfax, VA 22033
Tel: (800) 929-4040
Web site: www.foodallergy.org
A national organization that provides information on food allergies to sufferers and their families as well as raising awareness through education, advocacy, and research efforts. The web site also provides updated information ingredient notices, recipes, and a separate section for children and teens.

US Food & Drug Administration Center for Food Safety & Applied Nutrition

5100 Paint Branch Parkway
College Park, MD 20740
Tel: (888) 723-3366
www.cfsan.fda.gov
Protects the public's health and consumer interests. A useful website for understanding food labeling rules and regulations relating to food manufacture and production.

your own useful addresses

Use these pages to record addresses and phone numbers that you may want to keep a note of, such as your doctor, midwife, or breastfeeding support group, as well as useful web sites you may come across. It's handy to keep them all in one place.

Index

a

alcohol 28
allergies 14–16, 27–8, 63, 67
anaphylactic reactions 15
Annabel's chicken
   enchiladas 158–9
antibiotics 113
antibodies 14, 21
apples 63, 114
   apple & blackberry
      surprise 172–3
   apple & butternut
      squash purée 56
   apple & pear purée 58
   chicken balls with
      spaghetti & tomato
      sauce 154–5
   hidden vegetable
      bolognaise 126–7
   Moroccan lamb 170
   oatmeal with apple, pear
      & apricot 70
   orchard crisp 130
   poached chicken balls
      101
apricots
   Moroccan lamb 170
   my favorite chicken
      purée 72
   oatmeal with apple, pear
      & apricot 70
arugula, pasta with arugula
   & mascarpone sauce 41
avocado
   chicken & avocado wrap
      37
   purée 53, 59
   southwestern salad
      44–5

b

baby rice 52, 66
bag-baked salmon 34–5
baked cod gratin 31
baked pita chips 118
baked sweet potato purée
   57
baked sweet potato &
   spinach purée 69
baking vegetables 53

bananas 114
   bananas 'foster' 131
   bomb muffins 116–17
   cream cheese & banana
      sandwich 92
   frozen 84
   iced banana smoothie
      sticks 136
   purée 53, 59
   toasted peanut butter &
      banana sandwich 119
barbecue sauce 168
beans, southwestern salad
   44–5
beef
   chicken balls with
      spaghetti & tomato
      sauce (variation) 154–5
   Chinese-style beef wrap
      37
   cute cottage pies 169
   hidden vegetable
      bolognaise 126–7
   meatloaf with tangy bbq
      sauce 168
   my first beef casserole
      71
   sesame beef & broccoli
      stir-fry 38–9
beta-carotene 114
blackberries
   apple & blackberry
      surprise 172–3
   summer berry frozen
      yogurt 134
blood sugar levels 112
blueberries 116
   bomb muffins 116–17
   summer berry frozen
      yogurt 134
boiling vegetables 53
bomb muffins 116–17
bottle feeding 21, 23–4, 25,
   51
BRAT diet 114
bread & cereals 66, 86, 111,
   114
   baked pita chips 118
   French toast fingers 89
   muffin pizza with hidden

      vegetable tomato
      sauce 152–3
   see also oats; rice;
      sandwiches & wraps
breastfeeding & breast milk
   8, 9, 21–3, 25, 26–8, 51
   mother's diet 26–8,
      29–47, 48
broccoli 53, 68, 93, 113
   broccoli & cheese baby
      bites 93
   chicken, broccoli & snow
      pea pasta salad 46
   fillet of fish with cheesy
      vegetable sauce 74–5
   pasta salad with pesto
      dressing 156
   quick chicken risotto 123
   sesame beef & broccoli
      stir-fry 38–9
   tasty vegetable trio 68
butternut squash
   first fish pie 120–1
   pasta with simple
      squash & cheese
      sauce 123
   purées 56, 120, 123
   sweet root soup 32–3

c

caffeine 28
calcium 13, 26
carbohydrates 8, 26, 111–12,
   113
carrots 32, 148
   carrot & orange salad
      100
   cute cottage pies 169
   fillet of fish with cheesy
      vegetable sauce 74–5
   first vegetable purée 55
   hidden vegetable
      bolognaise 126–7
   mini chicken pies 160–1
   muffin pizza with hidden
      vegetable tomato
      sauce 152–3
   potato & carrot mash
      with salmon 73
   sweet root soup 32–3

   tasty vegetable trio 68
   Thai-style chicken with
      noodles 166–7
casserole, my first beef 71
cereals see bread & cereals
cheese 54, 66, 67, 86, 111,
   148
   Annabel's chicken
      enchiladas 158–9
   baked cod gratin 31
   broccoli & cheese baby
      bites 93
   cheese & pea orzo 122
   cheesy scrambled eggs
      97
   chicken parmesan 124–5
   cream cheese & jam finger
      food sandwiches 90
   cream cheese & banana
      sandwich 92
   cute cottage pies 169
   double cheese sandwich
      92
   fillet of fish with cheesy
      vegetable sauce 74–5
   first fish pie 120–1
   frittata provençale 42–3
   mini croque monsieur
      171
   muffin pizza with hidden
      vegetable tomato
      sauce 152–3
   Parmesan & herb pita
      chips 118
   pasta with arugula &
      mascarpone sauce 41
   pasta salad with pesto
      dressing 156
   pasta with simple
      squash & cheese
      sauce 123
   potato & carrot mash
      with salmon 73
   tasty vegetable trio 68
   tomato, sweet potato &
      cheese sauce with
      pasta shells 94–5
chicken
   Annabel's chicken
      enchiladas 158–9

chicken balls with spaghetti & tomato sauce **154–5**
chicken, broccoli & snow pea pasta salad **46**
chicken with easy white sauce **96**
chicken parmesan **124–5**
chicken wraps **37**
Chinese-style beef wrap (variation) **37**
egg fried rice with chicken & shrimp **165**
mini chicken pies **160–1**
mini croque monsieur (variation) **171**
my favorite chicken purée **72**
my first sweet & sour pork (variation) **164**
nasi goreng **157**
pasta salad with pesto dressing **156**
perfectly poached chicken **96**
poached chicken balls **101**
quick chicken risotto **123**
Thai-style chicken with noodles **166–7**
Chinese-style beef wrap **37**
choking **86**
cinnamon-sugar pita chips **118**
coconut milk
coconut rice pudding **131**
mango & pineapple tropical popsicles **174**
Thai-style chicken with noodles **166–7**
cod gratin, baked **31**
colostrum 21
constipation 114
cookies
ginger cookie shapes **129**
mini oatmeal-raisin cookies **102–3**
cooking
with children 149, 150

methods 47, 53, 67, 96, 100
cottage pies, cute **169**
couscous 83
seared tuna with coriander couscous **40**
cranberries, strawberry-cranberry popsicles **135**
cream cheese and jam finger food sandwiches **90**
creamy zucchini rice **97**
crisp, orchard **130**
crunchy tofu cubes **128**
cute cottage pies **169**

d
dairy products 26, 51, 54, 66
see also specific types (e.g., cheese)
diarrhea 66, 114
double cheese sandwich **92**
dribbling 85
drinks *see* juice; water
dyspraxia 112

e
eczema 14, 15, 16, 65, 67
EFAs (essential fatty acids) 9, 21, 35, 40, 43, 67, 112, 114
eggs 43, 54, 67, 111
allergies 16, 67
cheesy scrambled eggs **97**
egg fried rice with chicken & shrimp **165**
French toast fingers **89**
frittata provençale **42–3**
nasi goreng **157**
energy-rich foods 85, 111–12
equipment 7, 22, 85
essential fatty acids *see* EFAs
exercise 150
expressing breast milk 22, 23

f
family mealtimes 85, 111, 150, 179
fathers 24
fats 9, 10–11, 149

fiber 9, 65
fillet of fish with cheesy vegetable sauce **74–5**
finger foods 13, 83–4, 85, 86, 87, **89–93**, **96**, **99**, **101**, 148
first fish pie **120–1**
first fruit fool **132–3**
first vegetable purée **55**
fish 8, 9, 26–7, 40, 54, 67, 112, 114, 163
baked cod gratin **31**
fillet of fish with cheesy vegetable sauce **74–5**
first fish pie **120–1**
goujons of fish **115**, 139
see also salmon; tuna
fluids *see* juice; water
folic acid 13, 44
food allergies 14–16, 27–8, 63, 67
food intolerances 16
food preferences 9, 53, 67, 144, 182
fussy eaters 147–51
variety & new flavors 10, 65, 77, 79
food refusal 23, 113, 147–8
fool, first fruit **132–3**
foremilk 22
formula milk 21, 23–4, 25, 51
freezing & reheating food 18
French toast fingers **89**
frittata provençale **42–3**
fruit & vegetables
breastfeeding mothers 26
cooking methods 53
finger foods 13, 83–4, 86, 148
five-a-day 8, 10
fussy eaters 148–9, 177
ices & popsicles 84–5, 86, 113, **134–7**, **174–5**
irritant effects 15, 65–6
juice 66, 112–13, 114, 150
low-allergen 63
nutrient content 12–13
purées 52, 53, **55–9**, 61, 65–6, **68–70**
see also specific types (e.g., bananas)

sick children 114
fussy eaters 147–51, 177

g
garlic 65, 114
ginger cookie shapes **129**
gluten 54, 66
goujons of fish **115**, 139
grains *see* bread & cereals
granola bars **30**
gratin, baked cod **31**

h
ham
mini croque monsieur **171**
pasta salad with pesto dressing **156**
handwashing 85
herbs 65
hidden vegetable bolognaise **126–7**
hindmilk 22
histamine 14–15
honey 54
honey & soy toasted seeds **29**
hydration *see* water intake & hydration
hydrogenated fats 11
hygiene 18, 23, 85

i, j, k, l
ices & popsicles 84–5, 86, 113, **134–7**, **174–5**
illnesses 113–14
immune system 21
see also allergies
iron 9, 13, 27, 28, 38, 51, 66–7, 111, 114
juice 66, 112–13, 114, 150
kitchen equipment & hygiene 17, 18, 23, 85
lamb, Moroccan **170**

m
magnesium 13
mango & pineapple tropical popsicle **174**
meal planners
6–9 months 60–4, 76–80
9–12 months 104–8
12–18 months 138–44
18–36 months 176–81

breastfeeding mothers 48
milk feeds 25, 60–4
mealtimes 84, 85, 111, 150, 179
meat 66–7
see also specific meats (e.g., beef)
meatloaf with tangy bbq sauce **168**
messy eaters 84, 85
microwaving 47, 53, 67
milk (cow's) 54, 66, 150
minerals *see* vitamins & minerals; specific minerals (e.g., iron)
mini chicken pies **160–1**
mini croque monsieur **171**
mini oatmeal-raisin cookies **102–3**
Moroccan lamb **170**
mother's diet 26-8, **29–47**, 48
muesli **29**, **88**
muffins
    bomb muffins **116–17**
    muffin pizza with hidden vegetable tomato sauce **152–3**
mushrooms
    bag-baked salmon **34–5**
    cute cottage pies **169**
my favorite chicken purée **72**
my favorite frozen yogurt **134**
my first beef casserole **71**
my first muesli **88**
my first sweet & sour pork **164**

n

nasi goreng **157**
no-cook purées 53, **59**
noodles *see* pasta & noodles
nutrition
    6–9 months 51–4, 65–7
    9–12 months 85
    12–18 months 111–14
    18–36 months 147–50
    basics 8–13
    breast milk 8, 9, 21, 51
    breastfeeding mothers 26–8

vegetarians 111
    see also meal planners
nuts & nut allergy 15–16, 27–8, 54

o

oatmeal with apple, pear & apricot **70**
oats 105
    apple & blackberry surprise **172–3**
    bomb muffins **116–17**
    granola bars **30**
    mini oatmeal-raisin cookies **102–3**
    my first muesli **88**
    oatmeal with apple, pear & apricot **70**
    Swiss muesli **29**
obesity 11, 149–50
omega-3 essential fatty acids *see* EFAs
oranges, carrot & orange salad **100**
orchard crisp **130**

p

papaya purée 53, **59**
Parmesan & herb pita chips **118**
pasta & noodles 54, 83, 107
    cheese & pea orzo **122**
    chicken balls with spaghetti & tomato sauce **154–5**
    chicken, broccoli & snow pea pasta salad **46**
    hidden vegetable bolognaise **126–7**
    hidden vegetable tomato sauce **152–3**
    pasta salad with pesto dressing **156**
    pasta with arugula & mascarpone sauce **41**
    pasta with simple squash & cheese sauce **123**
    salmon, cucumber & dill pasta salad **47**
    Thai-style chicken with noodles **166–7**
    tomato, sweet potato &

cheese sauce with pasta shells **94–5**
peanuts & peanut allergy 15–16, 27–8, 54
    nasi goreng **157**
    toasted peanut butter & banana sandwich **119**
pears 63
    apple & pear purée **58**
    orchard crisp **130**
    oatmeal with apple, pear & apricot **70**
    pear & butternut squash purée **56**
peas
    cheese & pea orzo **122**
    chicken, broccoli & snow pea pasta salad **46**
    chicken with easy white sauce **96**
    egg fried rice with chicken & shrimp **165**
    nasi goreng **157**
    Thai-style chicken with noodles **166–7**
perfectly poached chicken **96**
perfectly poached salmon **100**
petroleum jelly 85
pies
    cute cottage pies **169**
    first fish pie **120–1**
    mini chicken pies **160–1**
pineapple
    mango & pineapple tropical popsicle **174**
    my first sweet & sour pork **164**
pita chips, baked **118**
pizza, muffin pizza with hidden vegetable tomato sauce **152–3**
poaching
    chicken **96**
    meatballs **101**
    salmon 47, **100**
popsicles & ices 84–5, 86, 113, **134–7**, **174–5**
pork
    meatloaf with tangy bbq sauce **168**
    my first sweet & sour

pork **164**
portion sizes 8, 11, 54, 85
potassium 13
potatoes 148
    frittata provençale **42–3**
    my first beef casserole **71**
    potato & carrot mash with salmon **73**
    see also pies
shrimp, egg fried rice with chicken & shrimp **165**
prebiotics 9, 21
processed foods 11
protein 8, 9, 26
purées 17, 18, 53, 54, 61, 65, 83
    recipes for **55–9**, **68–75**
    recipes using **93–5**, **120–1**, **132–3**, **152–3**

q

quesadillas **171**
quick chicken risotto **123**

r

raspberries
    first fruit fool **132–3**
    raspberry ripple popsicles **135**
    red fruit rocket popsicles **174**
    summer berry frozen yogurt **134**
red fruit rocket popsicles **174**
red peppers
    Annabel's chicken enchiladas **158–9**
    frittata provençale **42–3**
    hidden vegetable bolognaise **126–7**
    my first sweet & sour pork **164**
    nasi goreng **157**
    pasta salad with pesto dressing **156**
    southwestern salad **44–5**
    Thai-style chicken with noodles **166–7**
reheating frozen foods 18
rice
    baby rice 52, 66

coconut rice pudding **131**

creamy zucchini rice **97**

egg fried rice with chicken & shrimp **165**

nasi goreng **157**

quick chicken risotto **123**

s

salads **44–7**, **100**, 149, **156**

salmon

bag-baked salmon **34–5**

finger-size salmon fishcakes **98–9**

perfectly poached salmon **100**

poaching/microwaving 47

potato & carrot mash with salmon **73**

salmon, cucumber & dill pasta salad **47**

teriyaki salmon **162–3**

salt 10, 23, 54

sandwiches & wraps

Annabel's chicken enchiladas **158–9**

for breastfeeding mothers **36–7**

finger food sandwiches **90–2**

mini croque monsieur **171**

toasted peanut butter & banana sandwich **119**

tuna tortilla melt **119**

saturated fats 10–11

seeds 43

honey & soy toasted **29**

selenium 13

self-feeding 83–5, 86

see also finger foods

serving sizes 8, 11, 54, 85

sesame beef & broccoli stir-fry **38–9**

sick children 113–14

snacks 26, 27, 48, 112, 113

solids see weaning & starting solids

soup, sweet root **32–3**

southwestern salad **44–5**

soy formula 23

spinach 66

baked cod gratin **31**

sweet potato & spinach purée **69**

star charts 149

steaming vegetables 53

stir-fries 148

sesame beef & broccoli stir-fry **38–9**

strawberries

first fruit fool **132–3**

red fruit rocket popsicles **174**

strawberry-cranberry popsicles **135**

strawberry milkshake popsicles **136**

summer berry frozen yogurt **134**

sugar 8, 10, 54, 67, 112

summer berry frozen yogurt **134**

sweet potatoes

baked sweet potato purée **57**

my favorite chicken purée **72**

my first beef casserole **71**

sweet potato & spinach purée **69**

sweet root soup **32–3**

tomato, sweet potato & cheese sauce with pasta shells **94–5**

sweet root soup **32–3**

sweet corn

my first sweet & sour pork **164**

southwestern salad **44–5**

Swiss muesli **29**

t

table manners 84

tasty tuna finger food sandwiches **90**

tasty vegetable trio **68**

teething & tooth care 84–5, 112–13, 135

teriyaki salmon **162–3**

textures 83, 107

Thai-style chicken with noodles **166–7**

toast

French toast fingers **89**

mini croque monsieur **171**

toasted peanut butter & banana sandwich **119**

tofu cubes, crunchy **128**

tomatoes

Annabel's chicken enchiladas **158–9**

chicken balls with spaghetti & tomato sauce **154–5**

chicken parmesan **124–5**

hidden vegetable bolognaise **126–7**

Moroccan lamb **170**

muffin pizza with hidden vegetable tomato sauce **152–3**

my favorite chicken purée **72**

pasta salad with pesto dressing **156**

tasty vegetable trio **68**

tomato, sweet potato & cheese sauce with pasta shells **94–5**

turkey & tomato sandwich with honey-mustard mayo **36**

tooth care & teething 84–5, 112–13, 135

trans fats 11

tryptophan 36

tuna

seared tuna with coriander couscous **40**

tasty tuna finger food sandwiches **90**

tuna tortilla melt **119**

turkey

chicken balls with spaghetti & tomato sauce (variation) **154–5**

mini croque monsieur (variation) **171**

turkey & tomato sandwich with honey-mustard mayo **36**

u, v

unsaturated fats 10

variety, importance of 10, 65, 77, 79

vegetables see fruit & vegetables

vegetarian diets 111, **128**

vitamins & minerals 8, 9, 12–13, 51

breastfeeding mothers 26, 28, 32, 36, 38

effects of cooking 53, 68

sick children 114

vegetarians 111

water intake & hydration 9, 11, 66, 112–13, 114, 150

breastfeeding mothers 27, 28

watermelon, red fruit rocket popsicles **174**

weaning & starting solids 51–4, 65–7

food allergies 14–16, 63, 67

kitchen equipment 17

meal planners 60–4, 76–80

see also purées

weight loss, breastfeeding mothers 26, 27

wraps see sandwiches & wraps

y, z

yogurt 66, 113

apple & blackberry surprise **172–3**

first fruit fool **132–3**

ices & popsicles **134–7**

zinc 13, 36

zucchini

Annabel's chicken enchiladas **158–9**

creamy zucchini rice **97**

frittata provençale **42–3**

muffin pizza with hidden vegetable tomato sauce **152–3**

about the author

Annabel Karmel is a leading author on nutrition and cooking for children, and her bestselling books are sold all over the world. In 2006, the Queen made Annabel a Member of the British Empire (MBE) for her outstanding services to child nutrition. Annabel is well-known for providing advice and guidance to millions of parents on what to feed and cook for children, as well as getting families to eat a healthier diet—with an emphasis on fun.

Annabel has published eight books in the US, including *First Meals*—a complete guide to feeding babies and children, and *Favorite Family Recipes*, *The Mom and Me Cookbook*, and the *Toddler Cookbook*, which are step-by-step photographic books that teach young children how to cook. She has also authored a keepsake journal, *Baby's First Year*, for parents to fill in and record their baby's milestones.

In the UK, Annabel has her own line of food in supermarkets, as well as a line of equipment for making baby food.

Annabel travels frequently to the US. She has appeared on many TV programs including Regis and Kelly, the Today Show, The View, CBS Early Show, and Tony Danza. She is also a regular on the Martha Stewart Radio Show.

Visit Annabel's web sites www.annabelkarmel.com, which is packed with recipes and advice, and annabelkarmel.tv to see step-by-step videos of Annabel's recipes.

acknowledgments

Author's Acknowledgments
I'd like to thank Peggy Vance at DK for making it such fun to work on this book; Caroline Stearns for working with me and testing all the yummy recipes, and her beautiful daughter Aurelia who once again is a cover model; Dave King for his stunning photos; Valerie Berry for her food styling; Elizabeth Jones for keeping my business running while I wrote this book; Evelyn Etkind, my mum, for tasting my recipes—even the baby purées!; Marina Magpoc Abaigar and Letty Catada for helping me in the kitchen; Mary Jones, my loyal publicist; Dr. Alison French; Dr. Adam Fox, Consultant Pediatric Allergist; all the models; and the wonderful team at DK: Helen Murray, Peggy Sadler, Sara Kimmins, Esther Ripley, and Marianne Markham.

Publisher's Acknowledgments
DK would like to thank Chloe Brown for prop styling; Dr. Adam Fox, Consultant Pediatric Allergist at Guys' and St Thomas' Hospitals, for his invaluable allergy advice; Dr. Rosan Meyer, Specialist Pediatric Dietitian at Imperial College, for checking the nutritional information with a limited amount of time; Susan Bosanko for the index; Alyson Silverwood for proofreading; Andrea Bagg, Nicola Parkin, and Karen Sullivan for editorial assistance; Charlotte Seymour for help on photo shoots, Robert Merret for additional help with prop styling; and our models: Lexie Benbow-Hart, Lachlan Bush, Gracie Daly, Georgina Davie, Ava Felton, Humaira Felton, Lewie Gunter, Dharminder Kang, Jas Kang, Zen Kang, Amais Limerick, Esther Marney, Ruben Morris, Ruby Read, Charlotte Seymour, Lizzie Shepherd, Aurelia Stearns, and Simona Tigîrlas.

Picture credits
The publisher would like to thank the following for their kind permission to reproduce their photographs:
(Key: b- bottom; l-left)
Corbis: Lou Chardonnay 28; John W. Gertz/zefa 8; Norbert Schaefer 21bl; PunchStock: Photodisc 84
All other images © Dorling Kindersley
For further information see: www.dkimages.com